INVIT
to *insp*...

Convention

Corporate Function

Leadership Summit

Sales Training Event

Awards Ceremony / Banquet

College, University Guest Lecturer

Company Retreat / Rally

Seminar, Webinar

Staff Meeting

Bible Study

Cruise

CONTACT SUSAN   800.607.2535

SUSAN@SGSPEAKERS.COM

Video: *www.FinalExpenseSuccess.com/troy-speaks*

How YOU Can

MASTER

Final Expense ©

An Agent Guide to Selling
Final Expense Insurance By A
National TOP PRODUCER

Troy Clark, Ph.D.

Copyright © 2010 Dr. Troy Clark. All rights reserved.
3rd Edition 2012

Writings contained herein are from the author unless otherwise stated.

No part of this publication may be reproduced, stored in a retrieval system or transmitted in any way by any means - electronic, mechanical, photocopy, recording or otherwise - without prior permission from the author.

Characters of the stories in this book have been given fictitious names to protect their anonymity. Illustrative rate quotes are not based upon actual data. All Scripture references are taken from the 1611 King James Holy Bible.

DISCLAIMER: The information provided by the author, and finalexpensesuccess.com, do not guarantee satisfactory results for individual agents or agencies who may apply any information in this book to their selling technique. All information provided is a suggestion, and may or may not be the best suggestion for the selling techniques and scenarios described. The business opportunities at finalexpensesuccess.com described are ever evolving and may be structured differently at any given time. Statistical data provided is current in 2009-2010.

Cover Design by Santiago Lopez

ISBN: 978-1-48018-454-1

Other books by Dr. Troy Clark:
The Perfect Bible (*www.TroyClark.net*)

The secret to selling is to *sell the secret*.

(Explaining your product should sound like the "best kept secret" in the entire insurance industry. Make qualifying for one of your plans a "mystery of anticipation".)

Troy Clark, Ph.D.

www.FinalExpenseSuccess.com

DEDICATION

To Departments of Insurance
Who keep the best interest
of consumers first.

To Life Insurance Providers
Who offer a plan for the unplanned.

To Insurance Agents
Who serve the needy.

ACKNOWLEDGMENTS

To my parents, Jimmie and Karla Clark, who fronted the initial $300 for me to earn the license that began my insurance career, who also became my very 1st insurance clients. Without the backbone of your limitless, loving support, I would not be standing as tall as I am today.

To my personal team of life insurance professionals for whom this book was initially written -
You are a pure pleasure to work with.
Thank you for our daily partnership.
I treasure witnessing your growth and lucrative success in serving the needs of others. You deserve all the best!

To God above, who orchestrated my path into the insurance industry.
It is His "Unseen Hand" that connects thousands of clients to the benefits my company offers, one-at-a-time.

An Agent Cared

A family stricken,
Death has come.
One is taken.
The loss feels numb.

Were they prepared?
Here comes the bill.
Thousands needed
Adds a stout chill.

Who really knew
He was next to go?
Final Expenses transfer
Six feet below.

A hug, a Scripture, a tear,
Amazing Grace sung so dear.
A crowd shuffles graveside leaves,
As sympathy and debt meld here.

Alas! A welcome surprise.
Policy benefits arrive!
An act of love from the deceased,
Comfort he planned while alive.

The difference is,
An agent cared.
A policy written.
A family spared.

Who saved the day?
Insurance heroes!
In a single check
With several zeros.

Empowering life in death
Is a value agents share.
Why sell final expense insurance?
WE CARE!

Dr. Troy Clark   2010 ©

Agent's Creed:
The more people I help;
the more profitable I can become.

life ♦ insurance

1809, Noun

Providing payment of a stipulated sum to a designated beneficiary upon death of the insured.

Merriam-Webster's Dictionary
11th Collegiate Version 3.0, 2003 ©

RECOMENDATIONS

This book is the most precise, step by step handbook to success in the Final Expense market that I have ever seen. A new or experienced agent following the guides in this book will succeed beyond expectations. I heartily recommend Dr. Troy Clark's **How You Can MASTER Final Expense** *to any aspiring insurance professional, without reservation.*

Fred D. McClure
McClure Insurance Group, Inc., 1975-Present
Davidson County NC Commissioner 1994-Present
Life Underwriters Training Council Fellowship
Insurance Continuing Education Instructor
Nationwide President's Conference 4 Years
   #1 Salesman Southeast Region.
   $1,000,000 Life Insurance Production in One Month – 1985.

With this book, I have learned to consistently and effectively close sales . My record week is 22 sales, averaging no less than 10-15 sales per week! Thank you, Dr. Clark, I could not have done this without your book!

Wendy
Louisiana Agent on Dr. Troy Clark's Team
22 Final Expense Policies Sold in One Week.

This is the kind of book every agent needs to read – and the only one you will need to read to help you sell final expense life insurance. It is a masterful guide on how to find the right product, and the right market, and to sell with the right attitude. Troy, a master salesman himself, has done a fabulous job communicating it in a straightforward way.

David Curtis Smith
Benefits and Insurance Law Center, President
2010 National Association Health Underwriters Legislative Council, Chair.
NC Association Health Underwriter, former President and current member.
Continuing Education Provider, 7 states
Author, *150 Days: A Photographic Journey*

This is the "missing book" for the Final Expense insurance professional – a complete guide, from licensing to selling to becoming a Top Producer. This book tells you what works and what doesn't and why – not just theory, but filled with practical field-tested scripts. Dr. Clark has done an outstanding job!

Tony
Texas Agent on Dr. Troy Clark's Team
Designer of Premium Rate Calculators for 3 Final Expense Insurance Carriers.
NE Texas Better Business Bureau , Member
Certified Estate Planner & Senior Advisor

SPECIAL RECOMMENDATION

How You Can Master Final Expense is a must read for any agent marketing to the growing senior population. Troy Clark has provided a blueprint for success by giving both veteran agents and those who are new to insurance, all of the tools that they need to thrive in a market where it is estimated that 10,000 people are turning 65 every day. I know of no other book in our industry that is as informative and as instructive as Dr. Clark's book, and I am happy to recommend it for anyone who wants to succeed in the Final Expense arena.

Lee Mowry, CLU, CSA
"Father of Final Expense Insurance"
Developer of final expense products
42+ years insurance longevity
Former Vice President Marketing for
Shenandoah Life, Integon Life and Occidental Life of NC

PREFACE

It has been said, true love is seeing another person's needs, as important as your own.

While most insurance agents relish the opportunity to make a lot of money, few highly successful agents relish the privilege to *serve* people in need.

The difference to being successful as a professional salesperson is the approach to a potential client. Selling is a form of serving.

A servant disposition ensures another person's need is met first before you get what you want. The more needs of others you fill, the more valuable you become to them, so the more business a customer will allow you to serve their family.

The key is to serve people who desire what you have to offer.

How YOU Can MASTER Final Expense is a book that will guide you, and your company, to a more fruitful insurance career on several different levels.

This book was written by my being constantly asked by insurance agents, business professionals, and friends, *"What is your selling secret"?*

By utilizing a "seamless" system of selling life insurance, along with a powerfully lucrative Sales Presentations Script MANUAL, at *www.FinalExpenseSuccess.com*, I have been able to best maximize my selling skill.

What you read in this book is the combination of my superior selling methods, my winning sales verbiage, and great detail covering every conceivable facet of serving final expense insurance the right way.

Read with blessing my own selling secrets, as well as the latest, cutting-edge selling system in the world for individual insurance agents.

There are a thousand different ways for any insurance agent to fail. So, to gain daily, profitable results, I present to you the most lucrative opportunity today in the life insurance industry.

Troy Clark, Ph.D.

4 Steps To The Sale

Make A Friend

Identify Need

Share Benefits

Close Strong

TABLE OF CONTENTS

20 Most Frequently Asked Questions — xix

Introduction — xxv

Chapter One — 1
Licensure/Contracting/Product/Leads
Commissions/Claim Payout/Compliance

Chapter Two — 33
Final Expense Field Sales (The Old Way)

Chapter Three — 65
Final Expense Phone Sales (The New Way)

Chapter Four — 145
Presentation/Schedule/Diet/Faith

Chapter Five — 191
Agent Pitfalls/Straight Talk/Can-Do Spirit

Conclusion (Your Final Expense Opportunity) — 245

30 Important Funeral Decisions — 255

Burial Expenses — 257

Endnotes — 259

Bibliography — 261

Contact Author — 263

20 Most Frequently Asked Questions About Final Expense Success.

1. **How long has Dr. Clark been in Final Expense?**
   Since 2003.
2. **What is the average annual income for insurance agents who utilize Dr. Clark's sales scripts, and sales methods?**
   Majority of first year agents utilizing Dr. Clark's sales methods gross a five or six-figure commission-based annual income.
3. **Am I ever going to run out of prospects to contact to make sales presentations?**
   No. Every agent receives a "Leads Companies Resource List". All types of leads, as well as a full spectrum of price points, can meet all needs and demands for each individual agent's prospecting and budget needs.
4. **How long does it take for a final expense policy to get issued?**
   It is commonplace for a "clean" policy application (healthy client) to be issued the same day a policy is sold! Otherwise, it typically takes a few business days, *not weeks*, depending on the insurance carrier.
5. **How long does it take for an agent to be paid commissions?**
   Commissions are paid immediately by the insurance carrier to an agent when the client's initial premium payment is made. It is commonplace for an agent to be paid commissions the same week, even within 48 hours a policy is submitted then issued. A client has the ability to start their coverage right away, or delay the first payment for up to 30 days.

6. **Does an agent need a non-resident life license for Final Expense phone sales?**
   Eventually, yes. You want to be able to sell in several states. ALL of your leads should access customers in the states you are licensed in.

7. **How many hours per day do successful Final Expense phone sales agents work?**
   Normal work day hours, M-F 9am-5pm. However, after becoming proficient within our system, experts working 6-8 hours per day, 4-5 days per week, often enjoy a 3 day weekend, while earning a six figure annual NET income!

8. **What kind of office equipment will I need to begin phone sales?**
   Telephone w/headset & 3-way call feature, computer w/internet access, an office space (home or outside business), $50 recorder, unlimited long distance phone plan.

9. **What is the upfront cost to get started?**
   $249.99   **Total Sales Success Kit** at: *www.finalexpensesuccess.com/total-sales-success-kit*
   Compare that to most Final Expense sales opportunities that require an upfront financial commitment for one agent between $1,600-$2,000.   OMG!

10. **What about the National Do Not Call Registry?**
    ALL LEADS in your own lead pool program should be scrubbed every 30 days against the National Do Not Call Registry. Some good IMOs do this for their agents *at no charge to an individual agent*.

11. **How many prequalifying health questions are there on the policy application?**
    Approximately 10, depending on the insurance carrier.

12. **Do chargebacks have a negative impact on commissions?**
    Not normally, IF an agent follows Dr. Clark's Sales Script to a "T". Our carriers report "well above average" Taken Rate (first premium paid), Placement Rate (2nd premium paid), and Persistency Rate (policies in force 13 months), when compared to all of their other marketing distributors – including field sales. Dr. Clark's Persistency Rate on all of the final expense policies that he sold is over 90%.

13. **Are agents "captive" to Dr. Clark's Final Expense organization for a certain period of time?**
    No. Agents operate their own Final Expense business on a month-by-month, week-by-week, day-by-day basis.

14. **Is there any *ongoing* training and support?**
    Yes. Weekly workshops are attended by agents all across the country, including the Top Producers in the country! You receive selling tips from highly successful sales agents, as well as get your individual questions answered. Weekly workshops are as Dr. Clark's weekly schedule permits.

15. **Can an entry level agent get one-on-one mentoring and coaching from the Top Producers in the company?**
    Yes! Dr. Clark personally mentors and coaches individual agents, as well as groups, via webinar, or in person!

16. **Is it possible to build a Call Center using a Final Expense system?**
    Yes! Simply set up an office space with the necessary equipment and plug into our phone sales selling system. We lay out each step of the way how this is done profitably. You may ask Dr. Clark to assist you in getting started.

17. How long did it take Dr. Troy Clark to write this book?
Nine months of writing, including all weekends; then 3 months of editing.

18. Can I refer other agents to FinalExpenseSuccess.com?
Yes. Simply let Dr. Clark know of an interested agent. If the new agent purchases a Total Sales Success Kit, the agent who refers a new agent gets a CASH Bonus, or discount!

19. Does the U.S. economy have a negative impact on selling final expense life insurance?
No. Final Expense sales experiences explosive growth within *any* economic climate. Our customers are able to make premium payments each month, because they are not "losing their jobs". The vast majority of our customers are either on Social Security or Disability. Since it is highly unlikely that the U.S. Government will pay $10,000 for every U.S. citizen's funeral, our product remains both economy and recession proof.

20. Would Dr. Clark provide Masterful Sales Training, or a Motivational Success Speech for my company?
Yes! From Top Insurance Corporations to mid-size and small agencies, Dr. Clark relishes the opportunity to positively influence any organization. Dr. Clark's personable way and positive presence impact multiplied thousands of business professionals monthly, to earn the title, *"America's Favorite Motivator"!*

Email: *hotline@FinalExpenseSuccess.com*

VIEW Dr. Clark's Sales Records & Production Reports:
www.finalexpensesuccess.com/career-bio

STOP giving your failures credit for making you Weaker.
START giving your failures credit for making you Stronger.

Troy Clark, Ph.D.

INTRODUCTION

Final Expenses are what it takes financially to bury the dead. It is expensive to live. It is also expensive to die. Every individual who dies will leave behind a financial bill that must be paid for by those kin or in closest relation to the deceased.

Death is coming. Each citizen, who will one day pass away, has an unspoken responsibility to make sure that this financial burden is covered before their death. Enter final expense whole life insurance.

If an individual does not have enough savings set aside to pay for their own funeral, a heavy cost then falls back on someone else to pay it. Check the national statistics (www.funeralplan.com), and you'll find that an average, decent funeral most anywhere in America cost $7,000-12,000. It is a responsible life insurance agent who warns a client of this inevitable future expense.

It is a strange but true phenomenon. Those who do not have much money typically buy final expense insurance more oftentimes than those who can easily afford it. The reason why is simple.

It is easier for the not-so-wealthy to pay a little bit at a time for burial coverage to have instant coverage, than it is to pay $10,000 at once from a savings pocket.

Oftentimes, wealthy people see little benefit for final expense coverage, if they already have an excess of $10,000 sitting in the bank. So, the clientele base of a final expense salesperson normally services those in the mid to lower socio-economic income bracket.

These are some of the friendliest, most grateful folks on the planet. My greatest joy as a licensed final expense professional is hearing many thanks from the family of a deceased client who previously put together a plan for coverage that paid out immediately upon the client's passing.

I also receive many kind words from a client who cannot afford a high coverage/high premium plan, but could afford a small, low-cost final expense plan with enough coverage to fund a decent funeral with pride. It satisfies an individual to know that they are able to fulfill this common end-of-life obligation.

An expert final expense insurance agent adds tremendous value to a client's life, as well as financial protection to a client's family in death. This is why we serve end-of-life benefits to those who need it most.

Chapter One

Licensure
Product
Leads
Commissions
Benefit Pay Out
Compliance

*Understand that you need to sell **YOU** in order to advance your career, gain more respect, and increase your success, influence and income.*

Jay Abraham [1]

Insurance License for Final Expense

To sell final expense insurance plans, an individual, age 18 and above, must earn a state certified life insurance license. This involves first passing a pre-licensing course to earn a pre-licensing certificate. The pre-licensing certificate then becomes your pass to be able to take a state life insurance exam. Once the state exam is passed, the state life insurance licensed is earned.

The traditional way to complete the pre-licensing course is to find the closest location to your area where typically a one week course is being taught during scheduled weeks of the year. This information can be accessed at a local community college, because the classes are oftentimes held there. Or, a simple search on the internet by Googling – pre qualify insurance classes and (your state).

The cost for a one week pre-licensing class held Monday – Friday is roughly $200-$300. All study materials are provided by the class instructor. Classes are characteristically 9am-5pm Monday through Friday. There is usually a test at the end of the week on Friday to determine whether or not you receive the certificate for passing the class.

It is also possible to complete the pre-licensing course online from home via the internet. By an online computer search for online pre-licensing classes in your state, many options will appear. The course material can be paid for, downloaded, printed out., and self-studied in the privacy of your own home.

The cost is about half of the cost of going to a traditional pre-licensing class($100-$150 approx.). There is typically no deadline to complete the course online.

The final test of completing to the course may or may not require being taken at a physical location. Depending on the insurance institute the agent chooses, sometimes there is no limit to the amount of times the agent may take the final test to pass it. A traditional classroom course typically gives only one chance on Friday to take the final test and pass it.

The certificate of completion to the pre-licensing course is presented to the individual agent on the same day the test is passed.

Assuming the individual passes the pre-licensing course with pre-licensing certificate in hand, then it is on to the final step of passing the state life insurance exam.

The state exam may be scheduled within 90 days of passing the pre-licensing course in most states. The pre-licensing instructor can give the agent information on how and where to schedule taking the state exam. The state exam cannot be taken at home or online.

Upon arrival at a specific date and time at the facility housing the state life insurance examination, the agent will need 2 forms of ID to enter. The agent cannot carry anything into the room where the state exam is being taken. Usually a free locker with a lock is provided just outside the room to place all valuables and extras the agent brought to the test site. The associates doing the check-in also will take a "mug shot" picture of each person individually who is taking the test to be utilized on the license certificate later.

There is no talking allowed during the test period. The time limit for taking the state life insurance exam is typically 90 minutes. There are approximately 60 questions on the life insurance test.

Upon finishing the test, the individual exits the room and retrieves his/her personal items. The test proctor will individually let each person know that they either passed or failed the state exam. No test score is given. Its either pass or fail.

If the individual does not pass the state exam, they may reschedule and retake the state exam up to 5 times total (depending on the state), while having to repay the state exam fee each time.

Upon passing the state exam, the newly licensed agent will immediately receive a certificate of passing on site to verify the state exam completion, until the actual state life insurance license arrives in the mail normally within 7-14 business days, sometimes longer. CONGRATULATIONS!!! You are now a member of the insurance fraternity.

Continuing Education (CE) is required to maintain a state certified life insurance license. Classes may be accessed online or in a traditional classroom setting. Traditional CE classes can normally be accessed at a local community college. A vast array of CE courses can be located online by Googling – insurance continuing ed (your state).

Within a deadline of 12-24 months from the date your license was issued, depending on the agent's resident state, a certain number of CE course credits must be earned. (In my state, it is 24 credit hours every 24 months) Full completion of CE credit requirements every 12 or 24 months for your resident state will guarantee an agent's individual license remains legal and valid.

If an agent has non-resident licenses in one or many other states, only an annual, or bi-annual, fee to the non-resident state for each one is required. There is not a requirement for CE course completion for non-resident licensure.

Errors and Omission Insurance (E&O), also called "professional indemnity insurance", is not mandatory to maintain a life insurance license, but it should be considered a necessity for the wise life insurance agent to purchase.

E&O coverage is insurance that a licensed life insurance agent has on himself for protection against being sued, or potential negligence claims made by clients. Policy amounts vary between one or two million in coverage. Monthly premiums can range roughly from $40-$140.

Most insurance carriers require an agent to have E&O coverage before or during contracting to sell their final expense products. Some insurance carriers do not require E&O coverage on their contracted agents. It depends on the insurance carrier.

Again, it is a wise investment for every licensed life insurance agent selling final expense insurance to posses E&O coverage, whether it is required by the insurance company you are selling for, or not.

Simply Google online - Errors and Omissions Insurance - to choose from a long list of providers. Two of the top E&O providers are Calsurance (*www.calsurance.com*), and NAPA (*www.napa-benefits.org*).

Contracting

Upon a licensed agent having the physical life insurance license in hand, options galore to contract with insurance carriers abound. It is extremely noteworthy to emphasize to any agent, especially a neophyte (newly licensed agent), that choices and changes later can be very costly.

To contract with an insurance carrier as an independent agent, or through an IMO (Independent Marketing Organization), several factors come into play for the initial agent investment. The reality is, it will cost an agent to start a sound insurance business, just like any other business. There are many factors to consider beforehand.

For example, if an agent contracts with an insurance company, or IMO who represents several insurance carriers, what are you (the agent) getting in return for signing a contract?

Does the IMO or insurance carrier have a successful selling system already functioning in place for the agent to "plug into"? Is there a cost-effective, exclusive and generous lead program that <u>matches</u> the product an agent will be selling? Is there initial, quality training for an agent, conducted by the IMO or insurance carrier? Is there any ongoing training or weekly workshops for an agent to participate in at no charge to the agent? Are the

Top Producers in the company available for individual mentoring and coaching? Do agents have access to a proven Sales Presentation Script? Are there advancement opportunities within the company for earning higher contracts, or to manage a team of agents in the future? Are there any agent incentives or bonuses in place for the agent?

Or, does the agent just get a lonely piece of paper representing a high contract without any value of the business tools listed previously?

Point is, when an agent is considering the cost of contracting, the appointment fees (a nominal one-time agent fee to contract with an insurance company), product supplies, office equipment, leads, sales producer equipment, non-resident licensing, etc., it all becomes apparent that perhaps switching insurance carriers and re-contracting later with another insurance carrier will always be a costly endeavor to start over. It is best for an agent to make sure that a decision to contract with any IMO or insurance company is well thought through.

Each change costs the agent. We believe that Dr. Clark's final expense opportunities will be the last change an agent will ever make.

Because we feel this is the last place an agent will park their carrier, every single item an agent needs, including exact verbiage to the customer, to generate one or more sales per day, is fully-functioning beforehand on our business platform.

There is no gap in our system. From the moment an agent is hired to the moment thousands of weekly income dollars grow an agent's bank account, every step is already in place.

It typically requires 5-10 days to complete our training, depending on how quickly an agent desires to begin. An agent may be in the "selling seat" earning sales commissions by Week Two!

An agent will receive commission payments from the insurance carrier that are deposited directly into the agent's bank account of choice upon the first premium payment of each client. This is all settled in the agent's contract with the insurance carrier.

An insurance carrier contract also establishes the agent as a 1099 self employed individual for tax purposes. Although we do not offer specific tax advice, the following are a list of tax deductions that an agent may inquire into, and perhaps take advantage of, under the guidance of a certified tax consultant:

    Car Mileage (Business)
    Business Meals
    Business Postage
    Tax Consultant Fees
    Incorporation Fees (Attorney Fees)
    Office Supplies and Office Equipment
    Insurance License and Continuing Education
    Errors and Omission Insurance
    Prospect Lead Costs
    Advertising and Marketing Costs
    Business Office Space
      (Square footage formula for home office)
    Business Telephone
    Training or Seminar Fees
    Other office equipment

The Product of Final Expense

Unlike scores of other insurance products, final expense life insurance is a perennial, low maintenance product.

There is no government specified "season" of the year to sell it. A favorite feature among final expense professionals is that it is simple to sell all year round, and easy to maintain for the client.

Have you ever tracked the number of client phone calls and visits to their local Health, Medicare, Long Term Care, Auto, or Homeowner Insurance agent? Approximately 75% of the combined contacts initiated by these insurance clients to an agent are requests made over fixing something in their policy that is not right to the client.

Agents selling these particular product lines constantly wrangle between clients and insurance companies, federal departments, doctor offices - ad infinity - over payment of invoices, incorrect information on client's insurance cards, underwriting discrepancies, information not received by the client as requested, transfer of car ownerships, bank draft delays and overdrafts, claims in jeopardy of being paid, as well as a whole host of minor details the client wants adjusted. These hair graying headaches are virtually **eliminated** in a simplified final expense product.

Once a final expense policy is sold to a client, the policy lays dormant, until the client's death. It just sits there. Sits there. Sits there. Sits there, and that's it. This is the beauty of it. Basically, the only time a final expense agent hears from one of his client's is if the client wants _more_ coverage (for the client or someone else), or to change a beneficiary, or of course, in the event of a death claim.

Typically, once a final expense policy is sold, I almost never hear from a final expense client. This is what I mean by a very low maintenance product.

The biggest difference initially is noticed in how final expense policies get issued by the insurance company underwriting department. Because we are merely considering a coverage amount to pay for a decent funeral and burial expense ($7,000-12,000 approx.), the initial underwriting requirements can be thoroughly and completely reviewed with the client in 10-20 pre-qualifying health questions on the application itself.

Ever seen the pages of detailed health questions on a Long Term Care application? Ever seen the pages of detailed health questions on any Health Insurance application? Mortgage Protection? Ever seen the pages of detailed health questions on a Medicare Advantage or Supplement application?

It only takes 5-15 minutes at the most to cover the 10-20 "Yes or No" simple health questions for a final expense policy.

The product questionnaires listed previously can take days, even weeks, to complete, depending on how much research is required of the customer to find their health history content, complete with a timeline!

Some of the most well-defined, yet liberal, pre-qualification questions of health are found in a final expense application. Unless a customer is in a hospital, using oxygen, diagnosed with AIDS or HIV Virus, or bedridden, most all customers can qualify for a 3-Tier level product.

The following list contains some examples of prequalifying health questions of final expense insurance:

> Have you smoked cigarettes in the last 12 months?

> To the best of your knowledge and belief, within the last two years have you 1) had 2) been diagnosed with 3) taken any medication for:
>
> 1. Heart attack, stroke, (TIA) mini-stroke, or angina?
> 2. Internal cancer, Melanoma, Leukemia, sickle cell anemia, or lymphoma?
> 3. Liver or kidney disease, or renal insufficiency?
> 4. Diabetes requiring the use of insulin?
> 5. COPD, chronic asthma, chronic bronchitis, or emphysema?

> Have you ever had a lung, heart, or liver transplant?

> Are you on medication for depression, schizophrenia, or neurological disorders?

> Do you have Parkinson's Disease or seizures?

> Have you had any life insurance application declined or refused for any reason in the past two years?

> Have you been legally convicted of a felony, or received treatment for alcohol or drug abuse?

Licensure/Contracting/Product/Leads/Commissions ... 13

"Knock-Out" Questions are those health questions that will disqualify a client for any coverage, if answered "Yes" to. Such as:

> Have you ever been diagnosed with AIDS or HIV virus?

> Are you in a hospital or nursing home, or are you confined to a bed or wheelchair?

> Are you using oxygen equipment for respiratory assistance?

> Do you have Alzheimer's Disease or dementia?

> Do you require professional assistance with Activities of Daily Living (ADL's): bathing, eating, or toileting?

To access superior life insurance products that COVER any customer w/the above physical challenges, purchase Dr. Clark's Life Insurance Carriers product at **www.finalexpensesuccess.com/life-insurance-companies**

It is not very difficult to cover final expense health questions, quote benefits, prequalify coverage, sell, and even *issue* a policy on the spot in the initial interview with a client, in about the same time it would take to enjoy a full course meal at a restaurant.

An agent submitting a clean (healthy client) application to the insurance company with an immediate bank draft on the first premium is normally paid commission the same week the policy is sold.

Because these very few health questions normally go back 2-5 years on the health history of the customer, the final expense underwriting department can issue a policy quicker than those of large life insurance policies, Health insurance, Long Term Care, and Medicare plans.

The underwriting department of a final expense insurance company will do a standard Medical Information Bureau (MIB) check on the proposed client, going back a few years on health records. In addition, some life insurance companies also require a Rx Prescription check, to learn what medicines the proposed insured have been prescribed in recent years.

This ensures a well-researched decision on the part of the insurance company to be able to issue the policy sooner than later.

All medical checks on the client are done up front at the time the application is submitted and the policy is issued. This is important! There is generally no medical check on the client on the back end of the policy at the time of the client's passing, unless the carrier sees a "red flag" reason within the 2 year contestability period. That is why the benefit coverage goes out so quickly to the beneficiary (usually within 48 hours to 5 business days of presenting the death certificate).

The strongest selling point to the final expense product is that it will be the very first money a family will see when the client is gone from this earth.

Again, the coverage claim characteristically takes 48 hours to 5 business days to pay out all at once. Large life insurance policies exceeding $50,000 have been known to take up to 6 weeks to 6 months before the beneficiary (usually the client's grieving family) sees the first penny pay out. Why is that?

Extensive medical checks on the back end of large policies take a while. The insurance company wants to be sure that the insured was telling the truth about their health history at the time the initial application was filled out, before paying such a large lump sum of cash, $50,000 and higher.

Typically not so with final expense coverage. Benefits pay out immediately. No medical checks on the back end of the policy, unless the carrier detects a "red flag" within the 2 year contestability period. Otherwise, no fuss. Just 100% cash at once in the beneficiary's hand by check during the worst week of a family's life. What a blessing!

Extra, no-cost benefits added to an issued final expense policy are a tremendous tool for the savvy sales expert. Depending on the insurance company, and their final expense product, an agent can share information about no-cost benefits available to the customer.

Connecting no-cost benefits to a particular need or lifestyle of the client is a skill to employ that guarantees you will master final expense insurance sales. The more an expert agent provides real life solutions to the client, the more policies are sold.

Examples:

A) A final expense product may offer an accidental death benefit (coverage amount automatically doubles if the insured passes away due to an accident). **Listen for lifestyles habits or recent accidents** that are hazardous to the customer (i.e.: motor cycle riding, cleaning chimneys, electrical work, slipping in the shower, trip down stairs, driving in snow and ice, working on a farm). Connect the dots for the customer. Tell them how this plan for coverage will DOUBLE coverage and protect their family even more in the tragic event of an accidental death. Example: A $5,000 plan goes to $10,000 without having to apply for it.

B) A final expense product may offer a no-cost cash value benefit that will pay premiums for the customer in case of a financial emergency. **Listen for past regrets of the customer in losing a spouse's policy for lack of funds, then not having the ability to pay for their funeral.** Ease a customer's distress by sharing with the customer that they can avoid this happening in their family again, because the cash value will build up to the point of being able to pay premiums in case the client is not able to do so, until the cash value is liquidated. This ensures a customer does not lose their protection, if they can't afford or miss a payment.

C) A No-cost Cash Draft Benefit allows the beneficiary to go to their local bank and withdraw $1,000 immediately upon death of the insured. This is great to take care of

immediate necessities at a time like this, until the full death claim is paid within 48 hours to 5 business days.
This protects a customer's adult children, who may have a lost job, or is on Disability or unemployment, from having to beg for help or be at the mercy of a heartless funeral home.

Leads to Final Expense

*To access a complete list of approx 15 Lead Companies that best suits Final Expense sales, purchase Dr. Clark's Lead Companies Resource list at
www.finalexpensesuccess.com/lead-companies

    A lead is a lead is a lead is a lead. That is, a lead card is simply a lead. There is nothing magical or guaranteed in any lead, new or old. It is up to an agent's own individual skill set to convert a lead contact into an instant sale.
    A lead card is simply a written invitation by a customer to receive more information. When a potential client responds to an advertisement representing your business, the customer is simply stating their interest *indirectly* by sending a response back to the company, which constitutes a lead. There are many different kinds of leads. These 3 are the most prevalent in final expense insurance:

        Mailer Leads
        Auto Dialer Leads
        Internet Leads

    For our purposes, we will focus our attention on the mailer leads. In my professional opinion, internet leads are too costly for an agent to make a six figure annual income.
    An internet lead does not require much effort from the client to respond – just the click of a mouse. Little effort, little remembrance. If a client cannot remember what they did on the internet recently, the sale is doomed from the start. Thus, it becomes more difficult to recoup the cost of internet leads with fewer sales.

Also, internet leads are initiated by people who have computer access. In other words, the mid to higher income bracket. The vast majority of final expense sales are made with clients in the mid to lower income bracket.

A higher income bracket inquiry is usually collecting *information* through a lead. A mid to lower income inquiry is searching for a *purchase*. Thus, a higher income inquiry is less likely to buy, which is less profitable for the agent.

Auto dialer leads are illegal on a Federal level. Depending on the state, auto dialer leads may or may not be legal on the state level in your state. (State law supersedes Federal law, if State law rules after the Federal Law).

A customer responds to this lead by picking up their ringing telephone, listening to a voice recorded message, and then pushes a button on their phone to state an interest in being contacted. Again, little effort, little remembrance. It bears repeating that auto dialer leads are illegal on a Federal level at the printing of this book. I do not recommend them.

Hence, mailer leads. This is the lead system I highly recommend and utilize above all others at **www.finalexpensesuccess.com/lead-companies**

Thousands of our proprietary mailers go out strategically each month through a top, national Mailhouse Lead Company on behalf of a final expense agent. An agent should only to the states that you are licensed in. We mailed our leads into states that generate the highest response rates across the board, across the country.

Your lead mailers are mailed to a 1) specific age, 2) Income level, and 3) geographic demographic that represents your final expense product(s).

This ensures none of the lead mailers are wasted on the general public who is too young or too old to qualify for the final expense coverage, and not mailed to heavily-mailed-to cosmopolitan areas (large cities), or to the highest income bracket, who generally are not interested in *purchasing* final expense coverage.

The lead mailer duly informs the public customer regarding funeral and burial costs realities and that our "most benevolent" Federal Government pays out a one-time death benefit to the survivor of a married couple (which may only be enough to pay for the Preacher or flowers of a decent funeral).

The mailer also informs the customer further that they have an opportunity to inquire into life insurance protection from these costs available in their state.

Upon reading our proprietary letter, a client knows that they are responding to a life insurance policy with a premium. Yet, still our response rates are well above average.

The business reply card sent in by the customer arrives at the Mailhouse and immediately gets uploaded IN REAL TIME, according to the bar code connecting an individual agent with each lead. This constitutes a lead.

Leads upload in seconds, and are usually emailed by a Lead Company to an individual agent. I call these "A" leads. An agent enjoys accessing <u>exclusive</u> "A" leads in real time via the internet, from the Lead Company.

An ever-replenishing national pool older leads ("B" Leads) keep growing and growing the more an agent purchases fresh mailers each week.

"B" leads are accessed by a wise agent often. An agent will have more, fresh "A" leads pouring into their private agent portal every week as sales are made.

This creates a virtually endless supply of leads for an agent to never run out of prospects.

Dr. Troy Clark's weekly production of 14 sales per week was made up of 40%-50% **"B" LEADS.** Just because any lead is old, does not make it "unsellable". There are gold nuggets in those older leads. Things happen in people's lives within 30-60-90 days. Things change. People's lives change. They made need coverage now, even though last month they told you that they did not have any need for it. NEVER give up on a lead.

Delivering sales presentations to customers is what generates sales. My agents relish the advantage of being able to make up to 8 presentations per day due to growing their lead pool.

Licensure/Contracting/Product/Leads/Commissions ...   19

Being able to "get in front of" enough customers is key.
   ALL leads within your lead pool should be cleaned, or "scrubbed", every 30 days against the National Do Not Call Registry to remain in compliance with FCC regulations (Telephone Consumer Protection Act). There is usually no charge to an agent for a monthly scrubbing service, if your IMO is providing a "lead portal" to each individual agent.
   An agent can be fined up to $10,000 (or more) for calling on a lead that is on the National Do Not Call Registry. We avoid this mishap by making sure all leads are scrubbed by schedule every 30 days against the National Do Not Call Registry.
   Because our agents are trained to not call on leads after 90 days, unless permission has been given by the customer, an internal system of checks and balances dates and uploads current information about each lead.
   Then, if you work for an on-the-ball IMO there may be "BONUS" Leads available for top agents. Bonus leads are a pool of leads *less than 30 days* old available to top agent producers who qualify for them based on an agent's weekly production.

If an agent receives a lead card with the space for the phone number left blank, what should an agent do? Simply look up the phone number of the customer at www.whitepages.com. Before placing any call to the customer, email the customer's name, city, state, and phone number to your IMO home office, along with a request to "scrub" the phone number against the National Do Not Call Registry.

The contact name and phone number should be scrubbed at no charge. The home office may then send an email to inform the agent if the phone number is on the National Do Not Call Registry, or not.

Any professional agent would rather be safe, than to take a chance on calling any phone number that has not been properly and previously scrubbed. A customer's phone number on the National Do Not Call Registry should never be called by a final expense agent.

A "Live Transfer" lead is the ***ultimate*** final expense lead on the planet. This works well for both individual agents, as well as Call Centers. There are 2 Steps involved in a "Live Transfer" lead.

First, a licensed "Qualifying Agent" cold calls through a list of contacts generated by specific demographics of a typical customer:
- Age: 50-85
- Geographic area: Rural areas, not dense populations.
- Income Level: $15k-$50k

Dr Clark's Cold Call Lead Script:
www.finalexpensesuccess.com/lead-companies

As an interested customer is located, they are asked pre-qualifying age & health questions to make sure that they qualify for an insurance policy. Upon completing the pre-qualifying stage..

Secondly, a "Closing Agent" (who knows how to close sales) is waiting for the customer to be transferred to them within the same phone system, or over the internet, via a Live Transfer Lead Company.

LIVE Transfer Lead Companies are in Lead Companies Resource List:
www.finalexpensesuccess.com/lead-companies

A "Closing Agent" simply utilizes Dr. Clark's Sales Scripts to CLOSE that sale immediately! This method generates 10+ sales per week!!
www.finalexpensesuccess.com/sales-script-manual

Agent Commissions

An instant sale / instant commission nature of a final expense insurance sale means bottom line instant income for an agent. This quick payout reality is the most appealing aspect of a sales career in Final Expense insurance. Depending on the Independent Marketing Organization (IMO) an agent chooses to partner together with, life insurance applications submitted generate an agent's compensation by either *submission* or *commission*.

Compensation by *submission* means an agent is advanced a immediate payment by the IMO or insurance carrier each time a policy is submitted, whether the policy is issued or not, as long as the initial premium accompanies the application.

Most IMOs do not operate on this heavy cash-flow type of "submission" commission structure.

Compensation by *commission* means an agent earns payment by an insurance carrier when either

a) a policy application is submitted and the 1 premium paid
b) when a submitted application gets **issued** into a viable policy with 1st premium paid.

Agent compensation by the submission method is rare by IMO standards. The payout for the agent is immediate, upon submitting the application along with the 1st premium payment.

However, if the application is denied by the insurance carrier shortly thereafter and never gets issued, the IMO or insurance carrier is stuck with having to retrieve an agent's advanced compensation. The IMO or insurance carrier may choose to retrieve the advanced compensation from the agent's paycheck the following week.

The most common agent compensation payout is through the *commission* method.

Although it may a day or two longer for an agent to be paid on commission rather than the submission method, compensation is still much quicker than most all lines of insurance sales.

Health insurance, Medicare insurance, Property and Auto insurance, Long Term Care insurance, etc., pay out to the agent in weeks, even MONTHS, after one application is submitted to the insurance carrier. This is a gut-wrenching wait for an agent who does not have an already existing financial base to live on.

There must be a better way to sell insurance, and get paid immediately, by getting policies issued quickly. *Let not your heart be troubled.* There is!

Typically, an agent selling final expense policies on a fluid sales platform is paid IN THE SAME WEEK a policy is sold!! This is remarkable considering the insurance industry norm averages 3 weeks to 6 months for an agent to be compensated on one sold policy!

Agent commissions are normally direct deposited into an agent's bank account of choice from the insurance carrier. If an agent is appointed with and sells for more than one insurance carrier, it is quite possible for the agent to see commissions deposited daily from policies sold with different carriers.

Normally, an agent is considered to be a 1099 self employed individual for tax purposes by most insurance carriers.

The formula for factoring an agent's exact commission per sale, depending on the premium amount, will be displayed in this section later on.

However, for now a general rule of thumb is that the average agent commission per sale is $250-500.

When you consider that agents employed in a final expense system average one or more sales per day, an agent can literally watch their bank account grow each week by thousands!

A "cap", or compensation limit per sale, is wisely instituted between an IMO and insurance carrier for each final expense sales agent. An agent commission cap is generally a high, yet fixed amount per policy sold. This means an agent will not be paid commissions above the cap limit, regardless of the premium amount of the policy sold. This insures sound financial protection for the insurance carrier, the IMO, as well as the individual agent. Why? Chargebacks.

A "chargeback" is the retrieval of previously paid commissions to the agent by the insurance carrier. A chargeback is typically the result of sold policies that were later cancelled by a client, or declined later by the insurance company for various reasons, such as unpaid client premiums.

All final expense agents succeeding on our platform have a cap in place for the maximum amount of commissions paid on each policy sold, regardless of the premium amount. The cap remains the same for each agent, each policy sold. This protects an agent from the potential financial hazard of being paid thousands in commissions, spending it, and not being able to "pay it back", if need be, through a chargeback.

Insurance carriers typically pay agent commissions by giving a final expense agent 2 choices of compensation:

    As-Earned Commission
    Advanced Commission

The As-earned Commission Schedule awards agent compensation from a percentage of each premium paid by all clients of the agent. The exact percentage is stated in an agent's contract with the insurance carrier.

When a client pays a monthly premium, the agent is paid a percentage of the premium as compensation by the insurance company. This eliminates any "chargebacks" later from policy cancellations, because the agent earns commissions as the client pays real-time premiums (as-earned).

Depending on the agent's contract agreement with the insurance carrier, the same percentage amount from the client's premium is paid to the agent each month. For example, if an agent's As-earned Commission Schedule is 100% in year one of the contract, the agent will be paid 100% of all monthly premiums paid by the agent's clientele base for the first year the policy is in force (12 months). Subsequent years thereafter typically pay a smaller percentage of the premium amount.

It may take years or decades for an agent to build a clientele base large enough to generate a six figure income based upon an As-earned Commission Schedule.

The second option is Advanced commissions. All agents within our organization are paid by an Advanced Commission Schedule.

An Advanced commission is immediately more lucrative than As-earned commissions. This allows the agent to build a solid financial base for their insurance business in terms of weeks or months, not years.

For an entry level agent wanting to build a local team of agents in the near future, the income potential to do so is realized in the matter of a few short weeks or months.

The actual compensation amount of Advanced commissions grants the agent up to 6-12 months worth of agent "advanced" premium compensations (as a loan) from just one premium payment (the first payment) by the client. If the client cancels, loses, or declines their policy within 1-12 months after the Advance commission is paid, the "advanced" commission is retrieved by the insurance company at the next pay period the following week, called a "chargeback".

Chargebacks are a financial reality, but not a hazardous threat at all to any agent consistently producing on our final expense platform. A Chargeback may occur occasionally. It is certainly not the norm, when you consider the Persistency Rate (percentage of policies that stay in force) is no less than 85% companywide within my organization of agents.

Remember, an average agent commission per sale is $250-$500. A consistent agent averages 5 or more policies sold per week. One chargeback per 10-20 policies at $250-$500 is not missed too much from a $1,500-$3,500 average weekly income.

We feel that our commission cap along with our Agent Commission Schedule is both fair and lucrative, protecting the agent, the IMO, and the insurance carrier from too much debt, or poorly written business. The solid performance of an unlimited lead resource, superior Sales Presentation Script, strong product, immediate application submission, and real-time commissions are set above and beyond financial reproach to all parties involved within a sound insurance company, or IMO.

An agent's contract level determines how much Advanced commission the agent will earn per sale. Below are examples of how to figure both the As-earned and Advanced Commissions.

As-Earned Commission:

$45   Client Monthly Premium
x100%   As-earned Contract Year One
$45.0   Total 1st Month As-Earned Commission

Advanced Commission:

$45   Client First Month Premium
x12   Months of Yearly Payments
$540   Annualized Premium
x100%   100 Point Agent Contract Level
540   Contracted Annualized Premium
x75%   9 months advance (75% of one year)
$405   Total 1st Month Advanced Commission

An agent also earns monthly income from premiums paid (renewals) *Note: The Advance commission is considered a loan by the insurance carrier to the agent, until the advanced commission is recouped by the insurance carrier from the customer's premium payments. Then, after that, monthly renewals begin.

As-earned "renewal" commissions then pay a percentage to the agent each month from all of his client's premiums. This is monthly income received, WHETHER THE AGENT IS WORKING OR NOT!! As long as clients are paying the premiums, the agent gets paid as-earned monthly commissions. This is called residual income.

An agent can receive residual income for as long as the agent's contract with the insurance carrier allows. With some companies, the residual income is for life, as long as premiums are being paid by the clients. Most insurance carriers allow a minimum of 10 years for residual income, commonly called "monthly renewals".

A little-known fact is that renewals are paid to the agent **regardless**, even if the agent changes professions. Monthly renewals are always paid to the agent, even if he decides to forgo his insurance license later, and do something different professionally. The renewal income stream still flows each month into the agent's bank account, even if the agent is no longer licensed or practicing insurance!

Theoretically, a final expense agent who consistently builds a solid clientele base may potentially retire within 5-15 years just from the monthly residual income alone! It requires determination to succeed year-in and year-out for at least half a decade to realize these terrific levels of income and financial solvency.

Benefit Payout (Claims) of Final Expense

The most promising value about serving final expense insurance is immediate benefit pay out to the client. Large life insurance policies exceeding $50,000 coverage have been known to take 6 weeks to 6 months (or longer) for the benefits to pay out to the beneficiary, because of extensive medical checks done by the insurance companies on health records of the insured now deceased.

Final expense benefits, on the other hand, which is usually $15,000 coverage or less, typically pay out immediately within 48 hours to 5 business days, because the pre-qualifying medical checks are accomplished *before the policy even gets issued*.

This way, the client's beneficiary receives full benefits during the worst week of a family's life to handle potential "nightmarish" funeral home scenarios, if the family does not have "cash in hand" to bury their dead.

My clients have informed me about funeral homes who would not allow their deceased loved one to be transferred from the hospital to the funeral home without upfront cash to pay for it. So, they had to "warehouse" their dearly departed in an obscure holding facility, until the cash was raised by the grieving family. The funeral home required payment or policy first before services were rendered.

A mid to lower income family need not worry about these tragic funeral home scenarios on top of all the emotional stress of losing a precious loved one who had coverage with final expense insurance protection.

The immediate pay out of policy benefits is the very last act of love by the deceased to his family, and a brilliant way for the insured to comfort the family. Even though gone, this coverage planned ahead of time by the insured blesses the family with financial security.

Several businesses unashamedly have their hand stuck straight out to a grieving family of the departed immediately following a person's death: funeral home, left over medical bills, nursing home care bills, credit card bills, debts, cemetery, etc. It is the duty of a sound final expense sales expert to warn of these realities and assist the client in choosing an affordable plan that covers all or most end-of-life costs, and above all else, fit comfortably into the client's lifestyle and budget.

Final expense insurance is the only business that does not take, but gives generously, at the time a family needs it most. Money is not everything. However, money is like oxygen. The more of it you have, it helps you to breathe easier!

A beneficiary simply may fax a copy of the death certificate of the insured to the insurance carrier, along with the policy number, to jumpstart the process of the claim payment. Within 48 hours to 5 days the full benefit payout is typically in the hands of the insured's primary beneficiary.

Compliance and Final Expense

There are people, believe this or not, with an axe to grind against anyone they deem worthy, who are looking for a chance to get an insurance agent into trouble with the Department of Insurance. It would satisfy these baser fellows to turn in an innocent agent to a state regulator over trivial, unintended mistakes on the part of an agent. The term "Gold Digger" comes to mind.

Mountains are made out of mole hills. Always bear in mind, whether selling insurance in a customer's home or over the telephone, what an agent says during a sales presentation can be recorded by a client unbeknownst to the agent. (Thank you modern technology made available to the general public.) This is highly unfair to the agent, but it happens.

An expert agent has nothing to fear who has nothing to hide. Every word and statement an agent makes with a customer must be inside compliant guidelines on both state and federal levels.

Selling Techniques to Avoid

Twisting involves convincing a client to replace an existing policy, or switch insurance companies, through misrepresenting the existing policy's terms and values. Never tell a prospective client that your policy benefits will do something, knowing that it will not do it. Never tell a prospective client that their existing policy will not do something without the policy in hand to review.

A **Rebate** is illegal for both the agent and the consumer. An inducement offered (anything of value) not specified in the agent's policy contract within an insurance purchase agreement is a rebate. It is illegal for any person to offer or accept such an inducement.

An agent may not charge in excess of the policy premium for the performance of the agent's service.

It is also a misdemeanor to the agent in most states to transact a contract that is unlawfully executed. That is, soliciting and transacting business with a non-licensed company.

Knowingly making false statements on an application is punishable in most states as a Class I felony. This includes insurance agents, physicians in charge of medical checks, or applicants of life insurance.

A blank application cannot be signed legally by an agent. Exceptions may be travel accident insurance, or a baggage loss policy, intended for issuance through a coin-operated machine.

Refrain from "hustling" or "badgering" a customer with untrue or unkind remarks, i.e.: "This is your last chance to ever qualify for these benefits", "Don't be a fool, sign up today", "If you wait another day to apply for this coverage, your chance will be lost forever."

Inherent within the insurance industry, unfortunately, are licensed agents whose only concern is to position a potential client to "sign on the dotted line" at all cost. To do so, a dishonest agent may withhold important, deal-breaking information from the customer about a certain policy feature that may influence the customer's decision one way or another.

For example, if a plan for coverage has a 2-3 year "waiting period" before 100% of the natural death benefits goes into full force, the customer should know this upfront during the initial explanation of the benefits. If the "waiting period" is not properly and thoroughly explained at the time of purchase by the sales agent, a family may get surprised by the sting of having a fraction or zero coverage they were counting on, if the client passes away during the 2-3 year "waiting period".

Up front honesty by the agent always wins more success in the long run. A customer is more likely to buy from a forthright, honest agent, who holds nothing back from the customer. There must be no surprises later to the customer or agent.

On the flip side of this coin is manipulating a customer to buy insurance based upon untrue or over-the-top explanations of policy benefits. An agent must never promise a customer that their policy will do something that it will not do. We officially term this "twisting" of the facts in insurance terminology.

Misrepresenting your product, or the product of another company that a customer is currently insured through, is detrimental to both parties involved and is no way to begin a lifelong, trusting business relationship.

If a professional agent is unsure how to explain policy benefits, or how to answer a customer's question about benefits, a correct response would be:

"That's a good question. Let me make sure I can give you an accurate answer by looking it up for you. Because I am a professional, I do not want either of us to be surprised later by giving you a guess answer. We'll come back to that later, I promise."

An Insurance Commissioner may revoke, suspend, or deny licensure to any individual for:

Cheating on the State Licensing Exam.
Fraud.
Misrepresentation of policy terms.
Violation of any insurance law.
Misappropriation of funds.
Conviction involving moral turpitude or any felony.
Violation of the Unfair Trade Practice.
Coercive or dishonest practices.
Forging names on an application.
Failure to comply with continuing education requirements.

Chapter Two

Final Expense Field Sales

(The Old Way)

*If you do what you've always done,
you'll get what you've always gotten.*

Anthony Robbins [1]

Final Expense Field Sales

The profitable method of serving final expense policies is to have more buyers requesting your professional assistance as a licensed insurance agent than you have time to get to. The key is to spend quality time selling, not prospecting.

The agent who is without a lead source from which to acquire clients is simply "cold calling". That is, drumming up business by word-of-mouth, or going door-to-door within a neighborhood soliciting business. Primarily, I recommend neither.

This is why as an entry level agent, it is a good idea to partner and contract with an IMO (Independent Marketing Organization) who already has in place the final expense insurance products, final expense lead source, final expense training and management structure that benefit agents who desire to sell final expense insurance profitably.

A high contract offer alone is not enough for an agent to succeed.

A licensed final expense *field* agent needs several items to complete one sale successfully.

The recommended list below represents essentials agent selling tools:

Phone with headset / Unlimited long distance calling plan.
Reliable transportation.
Professional business attire.
Map of county you are selling in, or GPS Navigation system, or Map Quest directions from appt to appt.
Zip-up notebook, includes: sales presentation, premium rate sheets, applications, agent state license, pic of your family, Memorial Guides, quote sheets containing 3 optional choices.

*Some FE carriers provide an agent an "E-notebook". Everything an agent needs to give a Sales Presentation, sign & submit a customer application is on the E-Notebook. NO MORE PAPERWORK!
GO TO Life Insurance Carriers List:
www.finalexpensesuccess.com/life-insurance-companies

Office supplies: pens (black or blue, red, highlighter / business cards / copier / alarm clock.
Weekly Leads (20-40 "A" Leads, approx 50-70 "B" Leads)
Weekly Schedule. (Chapter 4).
Appointment Setting Script. (Chapter 2).
Motel Reservations. (The local Chamber of Commerce can lend specific information on motels).
Bank Routing Numbers List, *www.gregthatcher.com*
An official clip-on name badge.
A sack lunch. (To save money!)

Appointment Setting

Nothing is more important to a final expense field agent than appointment setting. You can't sell a policy without people to present your product to.

No matter how high a commission level is offered by an IMO (Independent Marketing Organization), without quality leads and customer appointments, the highest contract is futile.

High contract + no appointments = zero sales. A 150 pt. contract is an extremely high contract, for example. However, without quality appointments for the agent to sell his product, 150 x 0 is still zero!

As an expert final expense agent, I much rather would prefer a lower contract (50-80 pts.) with an IMO who provided me with high quality leads for appointment setting.

As a first year licensed final expense field agent, I sold an average of 14 policies per week (669 new clients within 48 weeks), while being compensated by a lowly 50 pt. contract.

Everything about insurance was new to me back then. I had no clue this was an extremely low commission level. Yet, I was happy as a June bug on the last of May, because I was spending quality time selling, not prospecting for clients. I received 20-40 fresh, new leads each week, as well as 100 scrubbed, older leads (60-90 days). If I generated enough policies sold for the production goal of the week, I did not have to pay for leads. From this bulk of leads each week, I set my appointments.

As a field agent (selling policies in customers' homes), the key is to have more buyers in front of the agent each day than one can write policies for. On a typical week, Friday is when I would turn my production and paperwork for the week, acquire a new stack of leads, and also get paid. Saturday is my fun day. Sunday is my church day of complete rest (or writing!), which brings us to Monday – my appointment setting day.

Beginning at 9am each Monday, I personally would begin to call my leads and set appointments for Tuesday–Thursday. I recommend a telephone with a head set and an unlimited long distance calling plan, or a Sam's Club calling card.

Here is a helpful tip, if you are using your own telephone to set weekly appointments. You may want your **company name** to show up on the other side of the listener's Caller ID.

A customer interested in final expense protection may not, however, be interested in speaking to "Jane Doe" on their Caller ID, especially if the customer does not recognize the **agent's name**. You want to be immediately identified on anyone's Caller ID as a professional business, who can handle their inquiry into end-of-life benefits.

Many agents hire an appointment setter to work throughout the week calling ahead of the agent to set appointments for the next day. (This allows agents to play golf on Monday, instead of work) Not for me. It was more cost effective in my weekly schedule to personally set one day aside to set my appointments for the entire week.

Ever heard the saying, *"If you want something done right, you better do it yourself"*? How true. It probably worked to my advantage that I was previously skilled in communications by public speaking experience and private counseling. I set all of my own appointments (30 max) for the entire week within 4-7 hours each Monday. Beginning at 9am, I called through my leads several times over, until I contacted enough customers to set all appointments for the week.

I also believe by an agent personally making calls to the customer, a certain rapport would already be established with the customer, as I arrived for the actual appointment. This increased my chances to make a sale with a new customer.

View a simple appointment setting chart on the next page:

WEEKLY APPOINTMENT SCHEDULE

	SUN	MON	TUE	WED	TH	FRI	SAT
9:00							
10:00							
11:00							
12:00							
1:00							
2:00							
3:00							
4:00							
5:00							
6:00							
7:00							
8:00							

A weekly appointment setting sheet lay before me. This would become my official appointment schedule for the week. I called each lead, reading a certain appointment setting script that I developed, and share within my Sales Script MANUAL:
www.finalexpensesuccess.com/sales-script-manual

APPOINTMENT SETTING PHONE SCRIPT ©

Client First Name. (When customer answers the telephone)

Hi (Client First Name).

This is (Agent name)'s office with (Your Company Name). The reason for my call is, you recently sent a card back in to us requesting more information about our final benefit plans. The card briefly mentioned about plans you might qualify for.

So, I just wanted to call and verify the information here **you have given us.**

Our records indicate that you have not received the free information.

You gave us your date of birth as being_____. Is that correct?
Your correct mailing address is _____. Is that correct?
Great.

(Client Name), when the card was sent back it was filled out for (you / both of you). Were you primarily concerned with benefits on yourself, or did you have others in mind?
OK, great.

(Client Name), we do have that information available for you **this week.** This is a state regulated program in the state of ____ with immediate benefits. Since there is no physical exam, the guidelines ask that we see you in person to cover a few basic health questions to see what you qualify for. We have a nice representative in your area in (city) all day on _____.

What would be better for you, mornings or afternoons?
Is (time) o'clock ok?
Great.

The rep. who will be visiting with you, his/her name is _____. If you have a little piece of paper, could you jot down the name, so you won't forget about him? His name is _____. You spell it ------. He's a super nice fella', and we are looking at (time) on (day) to deliver the free quote information for you. He'll show you exactly what you qualify for.

(Rep. name) will be glad to help you any way that he can.
OK? We'll see you then at (time) on (day).
*Optional : (Rep. name) will have your card with him, so you can see it.
Thank you (Client Name). Have a blessed day.
Bye.

    As the customer and I figure out the best time for the appointment, their name is written down in the time slot they indicate within my schedule. I set 8-12 appointments per day on the hour every hour.
    Lunch break was a sack lunch during drive time between appointments.
    Without fail, I always write down the name of the person I set the appointment with, and the date and time I spoke with them to set the appointment. When I arrived for an appointment, if the customer claims no one here made the appointment, it is very powerful for the agent to be able to say, *"Yes, (client's name) set the appointment on (day) at (time). You can't recall doing this 2 days ago?"* This is how I salvaged many appointments that turned into sales.
    In the very beginning, I would set 12 appointments per day for both Tuesday and Wednesday, then set 6-8 appointments on Thursday. After about 4-5 months, I became more proficient at selling, so I set 8-10 appointments per day on Tuesday and Wednesday, generating the same average of 14 sales per week, **and was finished by Wednesday evening!**
    Half day on Thursday was for finishing paperwork. Friday was pay day, turn in the week's production at the IMO Headquarters, and receive new leads for the following week.
    My weekly appointment setting schedule became a well-oiled, highly productive machine. While working fewer hours than most agents (Mon-Wed), I outsold 98% of all agents within our national company, because I was organized, extremely focused, and sharpened every aspect of my sales presentation into a buyer-inducing perfect pitch.

Appointment setting is key. Any agent cannot make one sale without having a customer to present your product to. Appointments are king to the final expense **field** agent. The most important thing to remember about setting appointments is this:

Separate Invitation from Presentation.

Setting the appointment is ONLY about setting the appointment. The appointment setting conversation between the agent and the customer needs to be brief, exacting, and over in the matter of a few moments. This is not the time to "prequalify" the customer on the phone by asking health questions. This is also not the time to "prequalify" the customer's banking information. Avoid premium sharing, coverage amounts, or quoting rates over the telephone, while setting an appointment. Just set the appointment. That's it.

It the event a pushy customer insists on knowing the coverage or premium amounts that they may apply for, the prepared agent can give a couple of responses:

1. "Mr. or Mrs. _____, this is a state-regulated program. I have no idea what you qualify for, until I ask a few basic questions. I am extremely busy today, and every day, with several appointments. That's why we are setting the appointment for me to share with you exactly what you qualify for. I am a professional. It would be unfair to both of us if I guessed at your premiums over the telephone without knowing anything about you.
2. The premiums start at less than $1 per day. I do not know you personally, which is why there are some basic, state-guideline questions for us to cover, before we know exactly which plan you qualify for. So, what works best for you on Tuesday - mornings or afternoons?"

Final Expense Field Sales (The Old Way)   45

Another helpful tip in setting an appointment is to call out the customer's first name when they answer the telephone. Assuming a lead card has both spouses names on it, whichever one answers the phone first, call out their first name. (*I have embarrassingly call out the wife's first name when the high-pitched voice of the husband answered the phone – oopsie daisy! Apologies are always in order.*) Anyway, people respond more readily to their first name over the common telemarketer greeting: "Hi. May I speak to Mr. or Mrs. ___, please."

Again, it bears repeating. Most telemarketers say both the first and last name of the person they wish to speak to. It creates a common defensive barrier automatically in the mind of the callee. Instant warmth is generated by a professional agent who is calling out the first name of the customer up front.

In setting appointments with a customer, it is imperative for the agent to be sure all decision makers can be present during the actual appointment. If an elderly, single customer wishes to set an appointment, it would only be wise on the agent's part to ask if a son, daughter, or Power of Attorney needs to be present for a decision to be reached during the appointment, if the customer sees a plan that they want for themselves.

"Are you your own decision maker?", "Am I talking to the correct person?", "Is there anyone else who needs to be at our appointment for you to make a decision?" These are questions asked by an expert final expense agent, while setting the appointment.

These questions are designed to prompt a more clear explanation about the client's situation with regards to who makes the final decisions on the client's behalf. I would never set an appointment with a client, unless I knew all decision makers are able to be present at the time of our scheduled appointment.

Sometimes an extra phone call is required by the agent to a son, daughter, close relative, or Power of Attorney of the customer. The professional agent introduces him/herself to the person, and lets them know about the customer's initial inquiry into final expense benefits available in their area (the customer's response card), and would prefer to meet together in their presence as well, because you (the agent) require all decision makers to be present at the appointment meeting.

The appointment can <u>then</u> be set correctly with every interested and involved party, so that a decision can be reached together during the appointment.

It makes the customer and the customer's family feel better that a decision was finalized with all of them being present. This lends enormous credibility to the agent as a customer's family will notice the foresight of an agent to make appointment plans based on keeping the customer's family "in the loop". The advantage to the agent is that it dramatically increases the opportunity to reach a point of decision with the customer sooner on the actual day of the appointment.

If there is no additional decision maker other than the name(s) on the lead card, the agent is then free to move forward to set the appointment with the individual customer, or married couple.

Phone sales, on the other hand, does not require appointment setting. Leads are accessed online within a private agent lead portal and then called on by a licensed agent, to customers who actually prefer to do business over the telephone.

Directions / Motel Reservations

Now, my weekly appointment schedule is filled with 25-30 appointments for Tuesday-Thursday. Once my appointment schedule is set for the week by Monday afternoon, my gracious mother was given my schedule (she lives not far from me).

She would Map Quest directions from one appointment to the next appointment for each selling day Tuesday-Thursday, and then print them out. This was before I had adequate funds to purchase a good GPS Navigation System for my automobile. My benevolent mother did this for approximately 6 months each and every week. She was compensated nicely by her son.

Final Expense Field Sales (The Old Way)   47

I honor my mother, Karla Clark, and exalt her to the highest queenly level of praise for not only her professional assistance, but also her personal encouragement that guided me through the initial learning curve of this challenging new business venture of selling final expense insurance "in the field".

For me back then, it was a period of earth-shattering, personal hardship. My life was experiencing severe changes. It was a tough time, personally. Yet, final expense insurance field sales helped me to get through it. I owe my success to the joint team effort of my gracious, intelligent mother and I.

I write this book to "give back" to the profession that gave to me the chance to dust myself off, and get back on my feet again. Success is oftentimes birthed out of painful adversity.

The next task to complete would be making reservations for a motel room in the county I would be selling during the week. The local Chamber of Commerce in the county where an agent is selling will share helpful information on local motels, price range, and quality that an agent is looking for.

I recommending accessing the Chamber of Commerce website in the city an agent is selling for direct contact information. I set my reservations on Monday for the week, so that when I arrived on Monday night or early Tuesday morning, my room and board is already locked into place for the week.

"No Show" Appointment Plan

After motel reservations are secured, an expert agent creates a plan for client "no show" appointments (absentee customer appointment).

It is not uncommon in the course of 8-12 appointments per day for the agent to be "stood up" by customers a time or two. I ALWAYS prepare "Plans B & C" for this unfortunate circumstance. This allowed me to continue working, even though the customer was not at home at the time previously agreed upon. Herein lies a secret to success.

An average final expense agent may be clueless of what to do during the hour of a "no show" appointment. **The biggest mistake an agent can make in the field is to get off track in your daily schedule and lose selling momentum.**

It would be easy to look around and notice everyone else in society who is leisurely shopping, eating, playing, etc., while the agent is working. This seduction begs the agent to quit selling for an hour to run an errand, or pick up some snacks, stop and eat an ice cream cone, do some shopping, or visit a historic site in the area. This is a mistake.

It takes the agent's mind off selling, working, executing, and following through on the plan for the day. Some agents even <u>stop selling altogether for the day</u>, because there is ALWAYS something that looks better to do than work.

I kept myself on track with a simple solution. On my appointment setting Monday, the last task I accomplished before I went to bed was to organize all of my unreached leads (leads that could not be contacted on Monday). What I mean is this.

I would look at a street map of the county (paper or online map) where I was working. For the address of my first appointment, I would then locate 2 or 3 unreached leads in the same, local, street area. If the original first appointment turns out to be a "no show", I would then follow up with a visit to the unreached leads in the same area. This assured me that I was never without being able to contact people and make presentations to prospective customers who mailed in an inquiry for final expense benefits.

In other words, I always made sure that for each appointment, there were 2 or 3 "back up" leads ready to fill in the gap of my schedule, if need be.

This is one of the biggest, yet little known, reasons why I out-sold most all other agents each week. I never *stopped* selling, while selling.

Professional Attire

I have studied and adopted every conceivable advantage of what works successfully in selling final expense insurance policies. INSTANT customer rapport during in-home field sales is based largely on sight. "Looks" in our society is important.

As I dressed in all different kinds of outfits: dress, casual, jeans, T-shirts, polo, shoes, sport coats, belts, etc.; customers would complement one certain look the most. I began to take note of this outfit each time I wore it. This outfit consisted of black dress pants, white dress shirt, and an American Flag tie. I received a compliment on my American Flag tie virtually every house I entered, whether I sold a policy or not.

Would you believe I bought 4 of the same outfits: black pants, white shirt, American flag tie, and wore it every time, regardless of the weather? Why? It was an advantage to me, because I noticed customers appreciated that patriotic tie. It gave me instant leverage and access onto common ground with most folks I met for an appointment.

On the other hand, as I arrived at the driveway for a customer appointment one afternoon, Gene, a fellow sales associate was exiting the same driveway! He informed me that no one was home. No wonder. We had probably scared the customer off with 2 insurance salesmen inadvertently scheduling appointments at the same time with the same customer! We enjoyed a hearty laugh together over the mix up.

Nevertheless, as our cars stopped beside one another on the driveway, I observed something about Gene, as we rolled down our car windows to greet one another and chat. Gene was distraught.

Gene's middle-parted thick dark hair was disheveled, crisscrossing in the part, sticking out on one side like he just scratched the side of his head. His beard shadow looked a couple days old. His open collared shirt was unbuttoned almost half down his chest with 3 robust chest hairs sticking out. No tie. He appeared either exhausted, or just coming from a disco. Then he confessed, *"I just can't figure out why people won't buy from me. I follow the sales script in a kind, professional manner. I just don't have any luck."*

Luck did not have anything to do with it. It was his image. Like it or not, the Hollywood television and movie industry have programmed entire generations of Americans to believe perception is reality. If you do not LOOK like a professional, you won't be taken seriously as one.

My dress pant, dress shirt, and American flag tie gave me a perception that pleased the visual sensibilities of whoever I was speaking to about final expense protection. You bet I wore that tie every time! If you ever receive compliments from customer after customer about something done right in their eyes, doesn't it sound smart to adopt it into your selling technique? Whatever works for down-to-earth customers is also right for me *when I am selling*.

Local Directions / Late for Appointment

Another directional tip for the agent who has a tendency to get turned around in a new city is to look up the phone number of the local fire department before you start your day of appointments. Keep it handy, if you get lost. Firefighters are mostly helpful and friendly when you inform them that you are new in town and need to ask for directions over the telephone.

Many times, before I owned a GPS Navigation System, I would get up early and arrive at the local City Planner's Office at 8am (especially if the region was mountainous with hard-to-reach back roads), to ask and pay for a comprehensive street map of the county. The local City Planner always possesses great maps of the area. If you're nice, you might just get a county map for free.

Of course, there is always the local convenience and grocery stores who sell county street maps.

In the event you are late for a customer appointment, may I suggest by trial and error experience, to NEVER call ahead to the customer to let them know you will be late? I have had more cancellations over the phone in the early days of my inexperience this way. If you are late, even by an hour, just let the customer know when you arrive that you are extremely busy with 8-10 appointment today, and the previous appointment took much longer than expected. Perhaps a "special needs" customer required more time than usual due to a unique situation.

It should be clarified to a customer who may be a little "miffed" by an agent's tardiness that the most important person to me in the world is the person who sits directly in front of me during an appointment, I am a people-helper, and that person is now YOU. Each family that I deal with has different needs and situations. I am focused on yours right now.

Appointment Arrival

Upon arriving at a customer's home for an appointment, make sure that you are prepared. It makes a customer uncomfortable when they see an agent (who looks like a stranger) sitting in a vehicle in **their** driveway for several minutes fumbling around with papers, etc.

As you arrive in the customer's driveway, have your Sales Presentation notebook stocked with everything you need. Immediately get out of the car with a sense of purpose, and walk briskly to the front door

Your official name badge in plastic sleeve should be plainly visible on the **outside** on your clothing.

I always introduce myself at the front door by simply stating, *"Hi. I'm Troy. I have an appointment with you today."* Begin to wipe your feet, as if proceeding to enter. The customer will crack the door open for the agent, or say, *"Come on in"*, as a welcome.

Client Warm Up

Compliments are my verbal tool of choice for the initial ice breaker. *"My, my, I wish my lawn looked like yours"*. If there is a car being worked on, I ask, *"Who is the mechanic? Do you work on cars for fun or to earn income?"* If I notice a collection of some sort in the front room, I may say, *"Wow. What an impressive thimble collection. When did you start?"* To be an expert salesperson, **you** must initiate meaningful conversation by showing an interest on the customer's level first.

If a customer offers me something to drink or a snack or gift, I never refuse it (within reason). No matter what it is! This earns acceptance with a customer quicker than anything.

If an agent refuses a customer's "goodwill" offering for a beverage, etc., then the agent has robbed the customer of the opportunity to be a blessing. If the customer gets the slightest impression that the agent thinks he is "too good" for them, all bets for a making a sale are off before it even begins. Be brave, and say, *"Thank you. Sure, I'll take something non-alcoholic to drink. What do you have?"*

It never fails. Every customer needs a "warming up period" to chit-chat and get to know an agent better. In the course of answering their questions about who I am, where I am from, and what I do, an agent, too, is asking questions about occupation or retirement, family, recreational hobbies, what are they currently involved in, or do they babysit much for their grown children.

Sometimes a customer is not talkative and desires to get straight to the point of business. In this case, I still cheerily volunteer information about myself, my travels in their area, and what I like about their community. It is good to mention if I also have other customers in their city as well.

Regardless if a customer is "chatty" or not, I make sure that I establish myself as friendly, yet professional, in business. Then, I show the customer the physical card that they mailed in to my office after they filled it out and signed it. This validates the legitimacy of my presence in their home.

Sales Presentation

The Sales Presentation that I utilized "in the field" is formatted to a similar structure that we utilize in "phone sales". There is an initial opening, warm up, insurance license and insurance carrier identification, benefits explanation, 3 option free quote, close, and agent rebuttal to customer objections.

To pivot the conversation to final expense insurance after a 5-10 minute warm up period, an agent may say something like this:

Agent: *You know, most people usually want me to hear their story, or the reason that motivated them to reach out for my help. This is something I ask everyone. Tell me, what do you feel your needs are? What were your thoughts and concerns about your family when you sent the card back in to me?*

Client: *Well, when we saw the card, we were curious if it would help us. We just do not want anything to fall back on our family, if one or both of us should be gone. We want to make sure our burial is taken care of.*

Agent: *I could not agree more. It sounds like that you care about your family. You want to get something in place that is permanent, never changes, pays out immediately, and is affordable. Does this sound like you?*

Client: *Yes, it does. I just don't want my children to have a big bill put on them.*

Agent: *OK, I do feel comfortable moving forward with you folks, because you care about your family. I'll be glad to help you every way that I can, OK?*

Client: *OK.*

An agent should then immediately ask, *"May we move to the kitchen table, so I can open up my notebook to share important information you requested?"*

It has always been my preference to do business at the customer's kitchen table. The kitchen table is usually a place of good vibes. The kitchen is also a family decision spot. Important family time is spent around the kitchen table.

Your presentation notebook is your income earner. My first, black leather presentation notebook netted me over $60,000 annual income, until I wore it out. It is the lifeblood of the sales agent working out in the field.

The very first thing the client needs to see in your notebook, as you present the product, is your state insurance license. I always carried a _copy_ of my license, in case I was ever robbed or mugged.

You would be surprised how many agents _do not_ show the customer their state insurance license. It would shock you to know how many customers have told me that of all the previous agents they have dealt with over the years, I was the only one who gave visual confirmation of my license. Agent credibility in the mind of the customer is king.

Next, I allow the customer to view a page of photos of my family. This lends to the customer a warm feeling of traditional values that most people share. It also opens up a conversation about their own family.

On the adjacent page across from my family photos is a big, yellow smiley face, which says underneath: **I CARE**. Together, the family photo page and the "I Care" page transfer a heart-felt, basic level of comfortable dialog that "breaks the ice" when meeting someone for the first time.

I CARE

Final Expense Field Sales (The Old Way)

The next segment of an agent's sales presentation consists of information about funeral and burial costs, information about the insurance company, and the prequalifying health questions.

It is only necessary to spend about 2 minutes on the funeral costs and insurance company details. The health questions require a lot more attention. So, my transition was swift into letting the customer know that "I can only help you today, if you qualify medically for our program."

The number of health questions are normally around 8-15, "Yes" or "No" answers. This doesn't sound very lengthy, however a customer with major health issues require a more in-depth review. All prescriptions need to be assessed, placed on the kitchen table, and discussed, for the agent to get a complete handle on the health of the proposed customer.

Typical underwriting health questions for a final expense life insurance policy are as follows:

\> Have you smoked cigarettes in the past 12 months?

\> To the best of your knowledge and belief, within the last two years have you 1) had 2) been diagnosed for 3) taken any medication for:
  1. Heart attack, stroke, (TIA) mini-stroke, or angina?
  2. Internal cancer, Melanoma, Leukemia, sickle cell anemia, or lymphoma?
  3. Liver or kidney disease, or renal insufficiency?
  4. Diabetes requiring the use of insulin?
  5. COPD, chronic asthma, chronic bronchitis, or emphysema?

\> Have you ever had a lung, heart, or liver transplant?

\> Are you on medication for depression, schizophrenia, or neurological disorders?

\> Do you have Parkinson's Disease or seizures?

\> Have you had any life insurance application declined or refused for any reason in the past two years?

> Have you been legally convicted with a felony, or received treatment for alcohol or drug abuse?

"Knock-Out" Questions are those health questions that will disqualify a client for any coverage, if answered "Yes" to. Such as:

> Have you ever been diagnosed with AIDS or HIV virus?

> Are you in a hospital or nursing home, or are you confined to a bed or wheelchair?

> Are you using oxygen equipment for respiratory assistance?

> Do you have Alzheimer's Disease or dementia?

> Do you require professional assistance with (ADL's) bathing, eating, or toileting?

Featured benefits of how the final expense coverage plan works is next. These graphically enhanced pages are typically all provided by the insurance carrier for the agent. The colorful design and illustrations are eye-catching to the client and provide professional intrigue.

Most of the appointment time (15 minutes) should be spent explaining the benefits of the plan for the customer. I created my own list of the benefits that my plan featured, and went over each benefit thoroughly with the customer and their family.

My benefits page looked something like this:

Whole Life Final Expense Plan

Provides the following benefits:

Whole life coverage / Stays the same for life.

No physical examination.

*Benefits **never** decrease / Premiums **never** increase.*

Final Expense Field Sales (The Old Way)

 Policy cannot change due to health or age.

 Cash and loan value (up to 10% interest). Makes premium payments for you in emergency!

 Accident Death Benefit (policy doubles!).

Extended term insurance – "Automatic Option".

Quick claim settlement – 3.9 day average payout!

 4 Million plans in effect today.

    To quote the premium rates next, I utilized a 3 Option "Bronze, Silver, & Gold" worksheet. Oftentimes, while looking up the premium rates and writing them down on the worksheet, the customer would be anxiously watching, and I would be humming a quiet, upbeat tune. These few minutes build into a mounting anticipation for the customer.

    Nothing keeps attention focused on the task at hand like anticipation – *"What coverage can I qualify for, and how much is it going to cost me?"* -the customer is silently thinking, while I am figuring numbers and writing it all down.

    Many agents take this moment to ask if the customer has a valid bank account or beneficiary information. An agent who asks the customer personal information prematurely before the customer picks a plan becomes a major deterrent to the sale. Why?

    I only want the customer's mind focused on one thing at a time. If you clutter the customer's mind with an overload of 2-4 thought provoking questions, it may overwhelm the customer, causing them to get "spooked". Also, the customer may perceive the agent as being too hasty, which will most definitely kill the customer's trust in the agent.

The Close

The "Bronze, Silver, & Gold Sheet" is an extremely effective tool to utilize at the close. It makes the choices plain and simple for the customer to visualize and choose.

See an example "Bronze, Silver & Gold Sheet" on the following page that I utilized in delivering 1,100 quotes within my first year of selling final expense insurance to make 669 sales.

Final Expense Field Sales (The Old Way) 59

To Purchase "3 Option Quote Sheet" Go To:
www.finalexpensesuccess.com/sales-products

SENIORS MEMORIAL PLAN
FINAL EXPENSE PROGRAM

- ISSUE AGES UP TO 85 (VARIES BY PLAN)
- WHOLE LIFE RATES DO NOT INCREASE
- BENEFITS DO NOT DECREASE
- PLAN CAN NOT BE CANCELED DUE TO AGE OR HEALTH CHANGE

GOLD
Natural Death Benefit
Accidental Death Benefit
Age $
Natural Death Benefit
Accidental Death Benefit
Age $
Total Premiums $

SILVER
Natural Death Benefit
Accidental Death Benefit
Age $
Natural Death Benefit
Accidental Death Benefit
Age $
Total Premiums $

BRONZE
Natural Death Benefit
Accidental Death Benefit
Age $
Natural Death Benefit
Accidental Death Benefit
Age $
Total Premiums $

Agent Name:
Phone #
PLAN

A life Insurance Plan to achieve **Peace Of Mind**

It is best for the choices to be explained by the agent through an illustration that appeals to a customer. I enjoyed asking the customer about their favorite pie (apple, lemon, strawberry). This generates a good vibe of warmth to make the benefits sound inviting.

Agent: *Do you like apple pie?*
Client: *Sure!*
Agent: *Well, if I baked you a delicious apple pie, you don't have to eat the whole pie all at once do you?*
Client: *No.*
Agent: *Of course not. You can just take a slice now that you are comfortable with. If you want another slice later, you can always come back and get another slice of the pie later, correct?*
Client: *Yes.*
Agent: *Same thing here. You can take a slice of coverage now that is comfortable for you, and then if you ever want to get more coverage later, because funeral costs go up 5% every year (you may want look at this again in another 3-5 years), you can always come back to get another slice of the coverage pie later. Sound good?*
Client: *Ok.*
Agent: *Now, which one of these 3 options appeal the most to you right now?*

    I always make sure I emphasize the words **"right now"**. This lets the client know they have reached a point of decision. I want them to decide either way "right now".

    Customer objections to making a buying decision today are common place. I address specific customer objections, as well as effective agent rebuttals in Chapter 3 under the heading "Close and Objections".

    Once the customer or married couple has picked a plan for themselves, immediately rehearse and remind them (1) how quickly the coverage will pay out, (2) all the additional no-cost benefits included in their plan, (3) the coverage amount and premium price will never change from this day forward, and (4) that we will complete the application today.

    NOW, is the appropriate time to secure beneficiary information. In filling out the paper application with a customer, there are two bits of personal information that may challenge the customer: Social Security number, and a check for the first premium payment.

Final Expense Field Sales (The Old Way)

These two items I usually leave last, simply because they can be the most challenging to retrieve from the customer. If a customer has already invested several minutes completing an application with me, they are more likely to finish it, even if they have an initial objection to releasing their Social Security number. I let the customer know respectfully that this is the very last bit of information that I need to make the application a legal document and lock the benefits into place permanently for their family.

To give the customer a substantial reason to release their Social Security number for the application, it is good for an agent to ask tactfully:

Agent: *Anything substantial that you have secured in your life (car, house, other insurance, bank account) required your Social Security number. This number makes this application a legally accurate document. Do you want this document to be a accurate, Mr. Client?*
Client: *Of course.*
Agent: *Do you want the benefits to go to the correct person (beneficiary name) after your death?*
Client: *Yes, of course I do.*
Agent: *Well then, we are not playing games here. If you are serious about protecting your family's future, the insurance company must know that you are you. We need to verify your identity, so the benefits go to the right person. Your Social Security number directs your benefits to go to your family, if something should happen to you tonight. Your Social Security number makes this a legally accurate document. Now, go ahead and read it to me please, if you do not know it by memory.*

The final task for the agent is to get the check for the first month's premium. The following is an effective way to address the need for a check:

Agent: *OK folks, we are almost finished here. Your plan can begin today with a check for $42.35.*
Client: *We can't pay for it today. It'll have to wait until the 3rd of next month (April) when I get paid.*

Agent: *Absolutely. What I will do is make an official note here on your application that you want your plan to begin next month promptly on April 3rd. Is this correct?*
Client: *That's right.*
Agent: *Perfect! What we are going to do to put this into place for you on April 3rd is simply write a check for the premium amount - $42.35 – and then, we will "post date" the check by marking April 3rd in the date line. I will make sure the insurance company holds tight to your check, until April 3rd, so that everything start on time for you. This is the last thing we need to complete for the application to be processed and approved. Go ahead and get your checkbook. I'll wait for you.*

Most all customers at this point in the closing of a sale realize that they must pay for their coverage somehow. Most will go along with writing a check if the agent explains it in a positive light.

Agent: *Now, folks, I have included a discount in your premium rates for allowing your bank to pay your monthly premiums for you.*
Client: *Really? Thank you.*
Agent: *You're welcome. Your first payment by check will be received by the bank, so that they can send in future payments on the day of month you choose is comfortable for you. You will always have a record of the $42.35 in your monthly bank statement. Would you like the bank to stay with the 3rd of each month to send in your payments electronically?*
Client: *You mean the bank is going to make our payments? We don't have to send a check in the mail each month?*
Agent: *You are correct. I am going to set this up personally for you with* (name of client's bank). *It is a no-cost service with most banks. They will send the payment in for you, so that you never lose your protection coverage, because payments get lost or stolen in the mail. Make Sense?*
Client: *Ok.*
Agent: *Which day of the month works best for you?*

Final Expense Field Sales (The Old Way)　　　　　　63

Client: *Let's just stay with the 3rd of the month.*
Agent: *Super! I'll mark the 3rd of each month on your application here. Remember, you will always see your $42.35 payment sent in on the 3rd each month on your bank statement at the end of every month, ok?*
Client: *Ok.*

    I address more rebuttals over the Bank Draft objection in Chapter 3 under the heading *"I do not share bank account information."* Once the check is in hand, the agent will prep the customer on the 5-10 minute underwriter phone interview to occur next:

Agent: *OK folks, one last item to complete and then you are set for life. We are going to place a call to the insurance company so that the underwriting department can verify the health questions one last time, since we are not doing a physical exam. It shouldn't be more than 5-10 minutes, then I'm going to let you get back to enjoying your day. Who wants to go first?*

    As the customer's plan of coverage is finalized with the insurance company underwriting department and the customer, a thorough agent will cement the sale by sharing a Memorial (end-of-life-planning) Guide. These are usually sent to the agent by the insurance company supplies department beforehand. There should always be a couple Memorial Guides in the agent's Sales Presentation notebook for each appointment.

    It is not a bad idea for the agent to write down and then highlight the coverage amount, premium amount, and monthly bank draft date, inside the front flap of the Memorial Guide, as a friendly reminder to the client. A brief agent explanation of the Memorial Guide to the client:

Agent: *Your Memorial Guide is a professional booklet for you to write in. You can record all of your important legal and financial information, your funeral arrangements, as well as any last words or instructions to your family of how much you love them. Also, when you receive your policy in the mail within 10 business days, you put your*

policy together with you Memorial Guide, and keep everything organized in one safe place, so that (beneficiary) will know exactly what to do for you. This will be the very last gift of love on this Earth that will comfort your family when you are gone. This is my gift to you for allowing me to serve your family today. I wish you a long and prosperous future.
Client: *Thank you.*
Agent: *Now, Mr. and Mrs. Client, do you feel good about the decision you made today?*
Client: *Yes. Thank you for taking your time to help us. We feel good about you, and about the plan we have in place in case anything happens to one of us.*
Agent: *I hope to not have to deal with this again for a very long time, but when that time comes, I will be right here to step in and assist your family myself.*
Client: *Thank you.*

Now, get the heck outta' that house as fast as you can before they change their mind! (ha ha) It is a good habit to leave shortly thereafter, because the longer you stay after completion of a sale, the more a client ponders over what they just did with the agent, good or bad. So, leave. Even if you are invited to join the client's family for supper, it is best for business sake on this first day of meeting your client, to express deep appreciation and take a "rain check".

CONGRATULATIONS on making the sale!

Chapter Three

Final Expense Phone Sales
(TeleSales)

(The New Way)

*Experience gained through failure
is success,
if you adjust to work smarter.*

Troy Clark

Your Final Expense Phone Sales Opportunity:
www.finalexpensesuccess.com/total-sales-success-kit

Introduction

My heart goes out to the individual agent working out in the field. The challenge is daunting. Bi-polar weather patterns, absentee appointments (no shows), car depreciation, flat tires, rough neighborhoods, funny smells in customer's homes, pets using the poor agent as a climbing wall, skyrocketing gas prices, fast food meals and indigestion, days in hotels away from family, MapQuest directions scattered on the floorboard underneath a pink bottle of Pepto – all this to be rejected by an unsympathetic, short-sighted spouse who sees no need for your professional assistance with funeral and burial coverage to protect his family, even though they are without any life insurance.

There's got to be a smarter way to make sales. There is. Welcome to the new millennium.

By selling final expense life insurance over the telephone out of a business or home office, an agent can typically reduce their weekly business expense by about 75%.

Gas prices, hotel stays, restaurant meals, car depreciation, wardrobe updating, navigation systems, time and money lost on "no show" appointments, paper applications, etc. etc., are virtually eliminated.

Final expense phone sales (telesales) is the ultimate path to prosperously serving life insurance.

It is commonplace for a telesales agent to initially meet a customer over the telephone, make a sales presentation, sell the policy, complete a voice application, and get the policy issued, **all in the same day**, all in 1-2 hours. The agent can then focus right back on the next lead prospect. This makes it possible for any telesales agent to sell more than one policy per day, while generating thousands of dollars of income in a one week period, week after week after week.

There are specific techniques that are effective in sales to be articulated to customers. An inherent timing and essential sequence to how and when to talk about important aspects of final expense insurance coverage to a customer is key. The ebb-n-flow of a successful sale depends on an agent being able to understand this knowledge.

Selling life insurance over the telephone sounds easy. How could something so simple be difficult?

Although telesales defines "working smarter", I consider telesales to be *enjoyable* work, not miserable work. Everybody wins when you enjoy what you do.

Even though a customer may literally be several states away, a single sale requires tough skin, on-task focus, and the ability to smile all day long, even though an agent "meets" prospective clients over the telephone.

Each page of my Sales Presentation Script MANUAL: ***www.finalexpensesuccess.com/sales-script-manual*** is engineered (by design) to accomplish important "tie downs" for both the customer and the agent. The *big purchase* decision at the close is made up of several ***little decisions***, mutual agreements between customer and agent, called "tie downs", throughout the script.

A skillful agent allows the customer to secure information about end-of-life benefits, while securing the sale at the same time. Look for the "tie downs" on each page of our sales script in the form of questions to the customer. Never bypass them. It is CRUCIAL for both customer and agent to reach common ground and find progressive agreement.

This is what "tie downs" ultimately accomplish. These scripted questions are the key that unlock every door for both the customer and the agent to be able to move forward together. Always together!

It is the wise telesales agent who masters the small "tie downs" on each page of the script, rather than only focusing on the big purchase decision at the close. The purpose of each page within my superior Sales Presentation Script MANUAL, and an explanation of each "tie down" question, is located in Chapter 4 under the heading "Sales Presentation".

An agent cannot be in a hurry to make a sale. It may take 1-2 hours to complete one solid sale. (Making $250-

Final Expense Telesales (The New Way)

500 in 2 hours is not bad, eh?) However, an agent must not rush a customer, or speed through a sales presentation to be effective.

Through final expense phone sales, an agent is searching for someone who will give him the time of day, or listen to his sales presentation, from an endless pool of leads to call on. The key is nonstop dialing, talking, and presenting free coverage quotes for daily sales to produce a healthy 4-figure paycheck by week's end.

This is definitely being accomplished within a 4 day work week by first year agents!

The most difficult obstacle for any insurance *field* agent to overcome is not having enough prospective customers to "get in front of" to sell policies to. Most field agents spend the majority of their business finances, time, and energy, prospecting and marketing for new customers. Selling policies become the least priority.

This problem is virtually eliminated in a sound final expense telesales opportunity that provides thousands of leads to call on each day. An agent can employ himself every day, talking to as many buyers as he wishes to locate in an ever-expanding lead pool.

Because mailer leads are exclusive to an individual agent, you may spend quality time **selling**, not *prospecting*.

It goes without saying that telesales can be easily lumped together with telemarketing. While a licensed telesales insurance agent follows up on leads that a customer has mailed back to the agent stating the customer's interest, the unlicensed telemarketer is strictly cold-calling.

It is easy for a customer who receives a phone call from a licensed insurance agent to initially confuse the insurance agent with a telemarketer. This blurry line of identification needs to be addressed quickly and clearly by the expert telesales agent, so that the customer sets the agent apart from "another one of those darn telemarketers" in their own mind immediately.

My Sales Presentation Script MANUAL does just that:
www.finalexpensesuccess.com/sales-script-manual

Verify Customer Information

Not every lead prospect is waiting by the telephone at home for an agent to place the initial call.

For decades in the insurance industry, there have been multiple hundreds of thousands of dollars spent, and many hours invested in research by trial and error experience, for leaving a phone message on an answering machine that generates a return phone call of interest from a lead prospect. Most companies are without the ability to do so.

I have it within my Sales Presentation Script MANUAL: *www.finalexpensesuccess.com/sales-script-manual*

My 10-15 second answering machine message script is read by an agent when leaving a voice message if the lead prospect does not pick up the phone to answer the agent's call. This single message left by an agent generates a return phone call of interest normally within 24-48 hours!

I conservatively estimate that one-third of my own personal sales, as a Top Producer in the entire country, were a direct result of return phone calls from customers, after leaving a voice message on their answer machine. This is flat out powerful !!!

By dialing either exclusive, or our free "public" leads, an agent leaves message after message on answer machines if no one is home. This is what I refer to as "scattering seeds".

Call backs by interested customers, who respond to the agent's voice message, are sales beginning to bud. In the same day , an agent can sprout dozens of return phone calls from interested prospects.

The agent then focuses on "feeding and watering" the return phone call "sprouts" by getting together with those who have responded to the agent with a return phone call. In doing so, the agent delivers the free quote information requested by the customer on the lead card by following Dr. Clark's Sales Presentation Script.

This phone activity cultivates the fruit of a sale.

Upon the initial conversation with a lead prospect, the agent should transfer upbeat, positive enthusiasm over the telephone without being overkill. You want to sound confident, not shallow or overly-zealous. Remember, an agent relates to a customer using only one of the five human senses – the sense of hearing. An agent's success depends on how everything **sounds** to the customer.

YOU want to bring respectful, delightful cheer into a customer's world on the other end of the phone while sounding official. A caring, positive phone call of cheer adds immediate value to a customer's life, no matter what kind of day they are having, no matter if the customer reciprocates appreciation for the call or not.

The biggest factor for an agent to remember is that whatever the agent transfers over the telephone determines the customer's attitude toward the agent.

In other words, an agent must be sure to transfer enthusiasm (and value) over the telephone to the customer. A lack of enthusiasm by the agent on the phone will also transfer to a lack of enthusiasm by the customer. An agent must FIRST initiate positivity.

Your job as a professional agent is to leave your customer feeling better after the conversation ends, whether they bought a policy from you or not. The more an agent gets into the habit of treating all people in this high regard, the more sales will occur.

Why is this? People are attracted to upbeat individuals. I am not referring to shallow, overly friendly zealots - like a bad TV "liquidation sale" commercial. Just a positive, balanced professional attitude carries a certain tone of respect that goes with it. Customers can sense this OVER A TELEPHONE more than an agent realizes.

Believe me when I say, a customer can sense if an agent is down, not on top of your game, frustrated, or just "not with it", over the telephone.

I have always said to entry level agents, if you can read our sales script, and smile over the telephone for 6-8 hours per day, you'll be just fine. Your attitude, as an expert agent, is to be friendly and warm FIRST, to set an inviting tone from the beginning of the conversation.

I always grab the customer's attention first by using their first name (on the lead card) - *"Mary?"* A first name is what a person is most comfortable with and most likely to respond positively to. It also sets you apart immediately from telemarketers, who initially use both the first and last name --- *"Is Mary Smith available?"*.

Avoid using the term "insurance" immediately upfront when introducing yourself and where you are calling from. Life insurance coverage will be fully disclosed to the customer within the first few minutes of the conversation. It is not a good idea to initially turn off a customer's interest by a first impression of being a pushy insurance salesman. It is best to use insurance specific terms without the word "insurance" at the initial greeting.

This is an effective greeting when the customer answers the phone:

Client: *Hello.*
Agent: *Mary?*
Client: *Yes.*
Agent: *Hi, Mary. This is (Agent first name) with Final Expense information you requested in Frankfort County. How are you today?*
Client: *Fine.*
Agent: *Great. Glad to hear it. The reason for my call, Mary we received your card in the mail,......*

After my full upfront introduction to let the customer know who I am and why I am calling about life insurance (found later in this chapter), I will then verify the information on the card that the customer filled out (date of birth, address corrections).

This allows the customer to take ownership of their lead card. It may take a few seconds to jog their memory, but usually a customer can remember mailing the card only a couple weeks ago. This lends instant credibility to the agent. It is crucial for the agent to establish credibility upfront with a customer.

At times, a customer may simply request for benefit information to be sent in the mail. This is not the idea an expert agent should go along with, as the benefit information is based upon the customer's current health condition. An agent has no clue upfront about a customer's health who they just met over the phone. An accurate quote cannot be sent through the mail, but rather can be delivered verbally over the telephone.

Example:
Client: *Just send me some information in the mail.*
Agent: *Which plan here do you qualify for? I have several different-type plans for immediate coverage here at my department, which one is right for you? Which one of my plans do you qualify for?*
Client: *I don't know.*
Agent: *Well, I don't either. You see, this is a state regulated program, I have some guidelines that I go by here. I have no idea what you qualify for, until I ask a few basic health questions. Is this a good time for you?*
Client: *How long is it going to take?*
Agent: *Is there anywhere you need to be right now? Do you have any appointments today?*
Client: *Not this morning. I have to go to church this evening.*
Agent: *Ok. I want to be respectful of your schedule is the reason why I was asking. Do you have some quality time to share with me now, if I push back my next appointment? It shouldn't take long for me to deliver the free quote you requested.*
Client: *Ok. Go ahead.*

    A customer may not remember mailing the card. Perhaps it was mailed by a spouse, son, or daughter. If so, it is good to ask, *"Jim, since Mary filled out the card, should I be speaking with her?"* Usually a spouse will answer, *"Yes"*, to this question if he/she cannot remember the card. The phone is then transferred to the person who will likely be spearheading the decision for coverage.
    Sometimes if a customer mistakenly thinks an insurance agent is a telemarketer, the customer may play "hard ball" upfront. That is, to deny ownership of the lead card that they sent in. In doing so, a customer may

say, *"I'm not interested",* or *"I never mailed a card in to you."*

    A savvy agent **must develop** a skill to overlook the customer's "brush off" and create a sense of intrigue through a striking response. Here are three examples:

Example 1:
Client: *I'm not interested.*
Agent: *Ok. What do you want me to do with your personal information that you mailed to me?*
Client: *What personal information?*
Agent: *You remember filling out a little card a few weeks ago that you signed as…..and your date of birth you gave us…..and your address……and, of course you gave us your phone number….is this you?*
Client: *Yes.*
Agent: *OK. Your card arrived on my desk today requesting a free quote on state-approved benefits in* (city) *for funeral and burial protection, if you qualify. I'll do everything I can for you and your family, ok?*
Client: *Ok.*

Example 2:
Client: *I didn't mail a card to you.*
Agent: *You didn't?*
Client: *No.*
Agent: *Boy, this is dangerous to you!*
Client: *What do you mean?*
Agent: *Somebody is filling out your personal information (name, date of birth, phone number), and sending requests in the mail for our information with your signature on it. I wonder who that may be?*
Client: *I don't know.*
Agent: *Would you like me to report this to the Better Business Bureau on your behalf, and see if they would investigate who is doing this?*
Client: *What did you say the card is for?*
Agent: *The card simply requests a free quote on state-approved benefits available in* (city) *for funeral and burial protection. I am extremely busy and spend time with families all day long who need my help with this.*

Client: *Oh yeah. I think we did fill out this card a few weeks ago....*

Example 3:
Client: *I don't remember sending a card in to you.*
Agent: *I'm sorry. It's probably my fault for getting back late to you. I see that you mailed in your card --- weeks ago. There are so many families who request my assistance, in fact, I have several appointments today, but I just did not want to let you fall through the cracks here. I apologize if I am getting back late with you, ok?*
Client: *Ok.*
Agent: *Let's make sure I am talking to the correct person. Is your name...? Is your address....? The date of birth on the card that was filled out is....Is this you? Do you remember now?*
Client: *I think so. Yes, I sent that in last month....*

In the event the person is not home who filled out the card, I go no further. A follow up appointment is set for when the absent spouse or person who filled out the lead card will be home. Why?

An agent simply and greatly reduces the chance to sell a long-lasting policy to a couple without the spouse who requested your assistance being present. If the card was filled out for both husband and wife, it is safe to assume that they make their financial decisions together. To make an instant *yet long-lasting* sale, an expert agent realizes that both spouses must be on the telephone together before giving the free quote for coverage.

So far, the customer has validated their personal information on the card with the agent. In doing so, the customer has taken ownership of the card. Now, the customer can take the next step to initial ownership of the benefits they requested. This is accomplished by the agent through simply asking a question:

"Now, Mr./Mrs._____ were you checking into benefits for yourself, or someone else?"

99.99% of the time, the customer will say, *"For myself / ourselves."* This is key! The customer is letting the agent know that they are genuinely interested to move forward and receive information and assistance from the agent on some level.

If the response card was filled out with both husband and wife names, a married person desiring a free quote on end-of-life benefits available in their area, should be asked by the agent if their spouse is also at home now.

A question I *always* ask in this case is, *"Since the card was filled out for both of you, am I assuming correctly that you both make your financial decisions together?"* If the customer answers "Yes" (most do), the wise agent will not move forward at that time with only one spouse present, but will reschedule a better time to call back when both spouses can be at home together to share a later telephone appointment with the agent.

If both spouses are at home, I ask for both to come to the telephone, either each one on separate phones, or by way of speaker phone.

Same principle applies to a single, elderly customer who may need a son, daughter, close relative, or Power of Attorney, to help them reach a sound financial decision. A wise agent will not move forward in the sales presentation, until ALL decision makers are on the telephone together.

Absent spouses or family members, who normally help with making financial decisions, who find out later about a family member's decision to purchase coverage on their own from a well-meaning agent, will most likely "poo-poo" the customer's decision. An absent family member who has no clue who the agent is feels left out. Inside pressure from a trusted family member to cancel a policy will cause the customer to fold. The policy is cancelled. Now, the agent will suffer a chargeback, lose the sale, and return to "square one', all because an agent was focused on greed, rather than long term customer relations.

It greatly increases mutual respect between the customer, customer's family, and the agent, when business is conducted accordingly to what is best for the customer's family situation. It also greatly increases the agent's chances to earn the customer's business long term, as well as close the sale immediately, with all of the decision makers on the phone together. "Together" is a warm, inviting word, isn't it?

Who I Am & Why I Am Calling.

It is at this point that an agent needs to put both a sense of clarity and assurance into the conversation. To do so, an agent shares who he is and why he is calling.

After establishing (in Verify Customer Info page) that it is ok with the prospective customer(s) to move forward together, an agent may then proceed to shore up some credibility as a professional and begin to put the customer's mind at ease on a financial level.

I also eliminate any up front, typical request for quotes and information to be sent to the customer in the mail, before a customer can ever bring it up.

There are only 2 primary concerns in the mind of a customer: *1) What can I get,* and *2) how much is it going to cost me?"*

An unhealthy customer may feel a sting of apprehension about being turned down for coverage. A healthy customer is more concerned over their premium rates. It is not uncommon for some customers to initially want this information in writing, instead of over the telephone directly. Why?

The fear of being turned down or turned away is a primal fear of rejection. Nobody wants to look bad, poor, or uninsurable, especially in front of a licensed agent whom they have never met. It is an agent's job to squelch these fears of the customer.

On the other hand, many seniors (65 and over population) prefer to do business over the telephone. Senior women, especially, feel insecure about a 6 ft 2 inch 195 lb. salesman whom they do not know visiting them in their home.

Nevertheless, an expert final expense sales agent will address these matters up front to curb the apprehensions of the customer, and project a vision of the customer's opportunity to qualify for immediate coverage.

Here is a sample conversation between agent and a customer who has just expressed that they are looking for benefits on themselves:

Agent: *OK, Mary. May I share with you in ONE MINUTE, who I am, what these benefits are exactly, how you may apply for them here at my department, and then <u>you tell me what do</u> after that, ok?*
Client: *OK.*
Agent: *Great. Mary, my name is (first & last name). I am a Licensed Field Underwriter** (*Note: This title is approved for our telesales agents by the insurance carriers we represent.) *here at the Final Expense Department. I am actually the decision maker. I either accept or refuse applications on those applying for our state regulated benefits here.*
Mary, these are 2010 state approved CASH benefits that pay out 100% to your beneficiary – **listen very carefully** *– usually within 48 hours after death, to cover all funeral and final expenses. THIS CAN BE THE VERY FIRST MONEY THAT YOUR FAMILY SEES AT THIS TIME to cover all funeral and burial costs,<u> if you qualify</u>. I have no idea yet even if you do qualify. We'll know in a minute. These cash benefits do go through small, affordable, whole life insurance policies that are regulated by the state of* (state of the client) *for folks who live on a limited income each month. These are not your real big expensive-type plans, just small, permanent plans that never change and payout as quickly as 48 hours. Make sense, Mary?*
Client: *Yes.*
Agent: *Now, I do not send out any salesman to bother you. You do not have to go anywhere. I simply give the free quote right over the phone, which is the information you requested in the card you sent back to me. This includes the coverage amounts, the lowest premium rates, and all the additional No-cost benefits that are available in* (client's city) *right now.*

Final Expense Telesales (The New Way)

I'll give you about 3 options to look at for just what it would cost for a decent, basic funeral in your area. I will start LOW when I give you my quotes, because, Mary, this is not going to do anybody any good, if it is not affordable. That is #1. I'll do everything in my power to keep the premiums as low as they can possible go for what you want, ok?
Client: *That's right.*
Agent: *So, I'll start low and give you 3 options to look at. Mary, if you see something that you want for you and your family, here is how this works.*

*If you see something you want, and **if I feel comfortable qualifying you for it**, I will simply help you to apply for the benefits right over the phone. It only takes about 5 minutes to complete our little application here.*

Now Mary, YOU DO NOT HAVE TO SPEND ANY MONEY with me today, in order to apply for the benefits! I do not want this gnawing at the back of your mind, while I am talking with you. Everyone who I speak with is living on a certain budget every month. I realize everyone gets paid at different times of the month. I have the authority to set your plan into place to begin at the price and on the day of the month that is comfortable for you, OK?
Client: *OK.*
Agent: *You do not have to spend any money today, if you see some benefits that you want to secure permanently for you and your family. Alright?*
Client: *Thank you.*
Agent: *Now, if you see something that you want, and if I feel comfortable qualifying you for the plan that you want, my secretary will send you a Welcome Packet tonight in the mail. You should get your Welcome Packet by ___ (day of the week, 3-4 days out). In your Welcome Packet, you'll have all of my contact information, which I will give to you in just a moment, all the information about the program you select, and our FREE gift called our Memorial Guide (this is a professional booklet for end-of-life planning). After you receive your Welcome Packet, within 10 business days, your actual policy will*

arrive in the mail. Now, Mary, I make sure we get the policies sent right out to you. Mary, I want every word that I tell you to be validated on paper in front of you in black-n-white in your Welcome Packet by *(day)*, and then in your actual policy within 10 business days.
Then, you are set for life! Your plan is permanent, never changes, goes with you the whole way, and pays out 100% with 48 hours to 5 business days at that time.
 I realize, Mary, that I am jumping ahead a little bit, but I just wanted you to know the process of how this works, if you see something that you want.
Now, Mary is this what you were needing my help with for funeral and burial protection?
Client: Yes.

At this point, I almost NEVER hear the customer say that they would like the information sent in the mail to them. Why? Because, I just did a thorough job explaining *how* the customer will get everything in the mail they need in their possession for the coverage they want.
If the customer immediately states "Yes" at this point, the agent has a buyer on their hands 85% of the time.

*Note: My entire Final Expense Sales Presentation Script MANUAL is laid out in easy-to-read & print format at: ***www.finalexpensesuccess.com/sales-script-manual***

Warm Up

The *Warm Up* period does just that. It "warms up" the customer to the agent. A level of caring is also perceived by the customer as the agent seeks to understand their family situation.
The goal is to build immediate rapport here. An expert final expense phone sales agent learns all about the customer, and makes them feel that the phone call is all about them. After all, our life insurance profession is all about serving the needs of others. This is what the customer must feel.

A pen and paper should be on hand for the agent to start taking notes here. I personally print out the lead contact on my computer printer to take notes on at this point, since it already includes the customer's contact and date of birth information.

You will know if you are doing a good job as an agent, if you are able to write a short paragraph about each customer's life or family, who purchased a policy from you. If an agent is not recording information the customer volunteers, this agent is not paying attention to crucial customer information that will help make the sale.

An agent is not doing their job accurately, if the agent cannot look back to a collection of notes recorded on every customer. This is where it all starts.

Items an agent brings up for discussion:

    Family
    Occupation
    Recreation / hobbies
    Current news events in their state
    Reason for the customer's inquiry into benefits

It also pays to Google beforehand local news events in the customer's area or state before placing the call to the customer, to gain common ground of conversation at this point. Most people are usually aware of the headline news topics.

Try to open up a topic of interest with the customer who is untalkative. Give a listening ear to the customer who volunteers family information.

The customer may want to share a negative insurance experience from a previous agent as a way of venting, or asking for help. This a **perfect** chance to "save the day" for a reluctant customer and seal the sale from the very beginning of the conversation!

Upon listening to a customer's horror story of a poor insurance experience, it is a fitting response for an agent to say, *"Mary, this is exactly why I called today. I am so sorry that happened to you. May I fix this for you?"*

It is critically important that an agent "saddle up" with the customer here. That is, to move over onto their side. Picture if you will a chain-link fence dividing the customer's yard with their neighbor's yard – you, the agent. It is the agent's job during the *Warm Up* to walk around that fence to the front gate, open it, and step inside their neighbor's yard to understand how they live and be able to empathize with the customer's situation.

One thing I am going to specifically accomplish during the *Warm Up*, as I learn about the customer's situation, is to make a connection between the no-cost benefits of my product to specific things the customer tells me are important to them. Watch for this in the mock conversation below.

Here is a sample conversation between agent and customer after the customer has answered "Yes" that they desire my professional assistance for funeral and burial protection during the "Why I Am Calling" portion of Dr. Clark's Sales Presentation Script MANUAL.

Agent: *Mary, I build **meaningful**, life-long relationships with all of my personal clients. I like to know something about who our cash benefits are going out to. So, I want to know something about your situation, what you feel your needs are, and who I will be working with in the future to pay out the cash benefits to. I want to be on the same page as you are, going in the same direction. So, Mary, how long have you been living there in* (city).
Client: *All my life.*
Agent: *Wow. You just sunk your roots down and decided to stay, eh?*
Client: *Yes.*
(*Note: If the customer is originally from another area or state, I will ask what brought them to their current location.)
Agent: *Did you raise a family there in* (client's city)*?*
Client: *Yes. We have 3 children. 2 sons and a daughter.*
Agent: *Wonderful. Do they live close by?*

Client: *Yes. One son lives in the same city here. The other son lives about 30 miles from here. And, my daughter and her husband live in this area also.*
Agent: *It's great to have them around in case you need anything. And they can keep a sharp eye on you, right?*
Client: *Oh yes. Sometimes, if I can't do something around the house that needs to be fixed, one of my boys will come over and do it for me.*
Agent: *Mary, I grew up in a close-knit family. There is nothing like it. Your family is your greatest treasure on Earth.*
Client: *That's the truth.*
Agent: *Mary, do you have any grandkids to babysit?*
Client: *Yes! I have 7.... 4 girls and 3 boys.*
Agent: *Looks like the girls outnumber the boys for now. Mary, are you the built-in babysitter?*
Client: *Sometimes. They come over here after their school bus drops them off, until their parent's come to pick them up after they get off work.*
Agent: *Well, that keeps you young, eh?*
Client: *You better believe it.*
Agent: *Mary, remind me to share more of this later with you, but there is a state approved no-cost benefit that allows our coverage to extend to your grandchildren at no monthly charge, if you qualify for one of our plans.*
Client: *Really?*
Agent: *Yes, I can cover all grandkids age 17 and below at no extra charge, until they reach a certain age. It is available right now in* (client's city). *Remind me to share this with you when I share with you the benefits that you qualify for, ok?*
Client: *OK.*
Agent: *You have several grandkids, so I want to be sure to include our no-cost Grandchild Benefit into your plan.*

Agent: *Mary, you are 67 years young. Am I assuming correctly that you are retired?*
Client: *Yes.*
Agent: *I figured so. What did you do before you retired?*
Client: *I was a beautician. I owned a hair salon for about 26 years.*

Agent: *So, you made everybody look good.*
Client: *(Ha ha) Well, I hope so. I still have several customers who want me to cut their hair, or give perms.*
Agents: *Believe me, Mary, it's hard to find a good barber or hair stylist. Now that you're retired, what are your hobbies? What do you like to do for fun?*
Client: *Well, I like to make dolls. I give away little dolls that I make out of socks and yarn to needy children or people at my church.*
Agent: *That sounds like it requires a lot of patience. How long does it take just to make one doll?*
Client: *Usually if I stay at it about 4-5 days.*
Agent: *Mary, I'm sure your grandkids all have a special doll made especially from grandmother.*
Client; *Yes, I gave each one of them a doll on their first birthday. Some of them still sleep with their doll I gave them years ago.*
Agent: *Mary we haven't mentioned anything about your husband. Is he still living?*
Client: *No, he passed away 2 years ago.*
Agent: *Mary, I am very sorry for your loss. How many years were you married?*
Client: *36 years.*
Agent: *Congratulations. That is very rare in our society in these days. What was your husband's first name?*
Client: *Bill.*
Agent: *Well, God bless Bill's memory. Was he decent husband to your family?*
Client: *Yes. He was a good provider. We just did not expect him to go so soon.*
Agent: *If I may ask, Mary, what did Bill die of?*
Client: *He had an aneurysm to the brain with a stroke, then died a week later.*
Agent: *Wow. That must have been a lot for you to go through all of a sudden like that.*
Client: *Yes, it was. I found him in his bed passed out and couldn't wake him. So, I dialed 911, and they took him to the hospital, and he never came home.*

Agent: *Were your sons and daughter able to assist you during that time to help you make plans and prepare for the funeral?*
Client: *Yes, I told them what I wanted, and they took care of it for me.*
Agent: *Mary, that is encouraging. I wish everybody could say that. A lot of people who I help unfortunately have nobody to depend on or lean on. So, although it sure is painful to lose Bill, it sounds like your family was a source of comfort to you.*
Client: *Yes. They still are.*
Agent: *Mary, if it's ok with you, since I deal with grieving families a lot, may I ask, How much did Bill's funeral cost?*
Client: *I think around $11,000.*
Agent: *Did Bill have enough coverage to take care of the whole amount, or did you have to pay anything out of pocket?*
Client: *Yes, Bill had enough coverage to pay off the mortgage and most of the funeral – I think about $7,000. My children had to pay for the rest.*
Agent: *You mean about $4,000 to make up the difference, right?*
Client: *Right.*
Agent: *Was that hard on your children to pay $4,000 out their pocket? It would be for me. I don't have $4,000 just lying around in the sock drawer.*
Client: *Yes, it was a hardship on all of us. I wish they did not have that put on them.*
Agent: *Well, I commend you for sending the card in, Mary. Most people wait until it's too late. You are very wise for reaching out for my help. There is usually a story behind what motivates people to reach out for my help, and I thank you for sharing a little bit about yourself with me.*
Client: *Your welcome.*
Agent: *This reminds me. Mary, please remind me to check on a no-cost benefit to see if it available in* (client's city) *right now. Your children have access to $1,000 immediately after you passing, until the full coverage*

amount is paid within 48 hours. Your children can go to their local bank, does not matter which bank, and withdraw $1,000 immediately, until the full claim is paid 100% within 48 hours. That will eliminate any financial hardship on your family at that time, and there is no extra charge for this service. Remind me later to include this in your plan at no charge, ok?
Client: *OK.*
Agent: *Mary, if I did not get a chance to introduce myself, my name is (Agent's first name). I am the Licensed Field Underwriter here at the Final Expense Department in Frankfort County. I thoroughly enjoy what I do. I consider this to be a people-helping profession. I deal with grieving families almost every day and take a lot of pride in watching these cash benefits pay out during the worst week of a family's life. You already know Mary, when someone passes away, it seems like everybody has their hand stuck straight out during the worst week of a family's life – the funeral home, leftover medical bills, nursing care bills.*
Client: *You got that right.*
Agent: *We all know that it is expensive to live. It's also expensive to die. It is not something that "might" happen. It is something that is **going** to happen, and it is always best to be prepared ahead of time for it. It's always easier to pay a little bit at a time, than it is to pay $10,000 all at once. Would you agree?*
Client: *Yes.*
Agent: *Everyone has an individual, adult responsibility to make sure that we do not leave our financial burden behind on anyone else. It sounds like Bill did a good job for the most part to protect his family. I'll do everything I can for you, so that your family has no burden put on them by your passing. And, of course, it must fit into your lifestyle and budget first, ok?*
Client: *Yes, that's right. Thank you.*
Agent: *Mary, who would I be working with in the future to pay out the cash benefits to – someone you trust to take care of your funeral and final expenses. Who would be your primary beneficiary?*

Final Expense Telesales (The New Way)

Client: *That would be my daughter, Tamara.*
Agent: *OK. I am going to make a note here for Tamara. Do you spell it T-a-m-a-r-a.*
Client: *Yes. That's right.*
Agent: *OK. Mary, when I talk about to the benefits, I am going to refer to Tamara, ok? She will be the recipient.*
Client: *OK.*
Agent: *Mary, just so that I know that I am on the same page as you, do you have any life insurance coverage in force on you right now?*
Client: *Yes, I have about $5,000.*
Agent: *And, do think that this will be enough coverage for a decent $10,000 funeral?*
Client: *Oh no. Bill's cost $11,000. I know I need more than that.*
Agent: *You're right Mary. Most people I talk to already have some type of insurance coverage in place, but most are not* **comfortable***, until they have around 10-15- or $20,000 coverage, just depending on what kind of funeral you want.*
Client: *Oh no, I just want enough to bury me.*
Agent: *OK. I'll help you do just that. Now, Mary, I want you to know that your $5,000 coverage that you already have in place will not be affected by our benefits here. In other words, the one will not affected by the other. In fact, our benefits here will more than likely be the <u>very first money</u> that your family will see at that time within 48 hours. So, I just want you to know these benefits will pay in addition to your $5,000 coverage, and will not affect it whatsoever, ok?*
Client: *OK.*
Agent: *I'll do everything I can for you, Mary.*

At this point, the *Warm Up* has brought us to the point of identifying the customer's specific need for burial expense protection. The effective agent must bring a customer's need for final expense coverage to the forefront and anchor the sale to it.

Identify Customer Need

The customer's **need** for final expense protection coverage is what carries the customer's interest into the benefits, free quote, and application process, throughout the entire sales presentation.

Without a customer disclosing why they are seeking coverage to the agent, there is no chance of making the sale. To uncover the need, apprehensions, fears, or anxieties of the customer over funeral expenses, becomes a necessary skill to the agent.

When a customer expresses what they feel their needs are, the customer is actually ***selling themselves*** on the agent's product. THIS IS KEY.

Establishing a customer's realistic need is not only crucial to an agent who sells the final expense life policy, it is also crucial to a customer's ability to gain leverage over their own apprehensions of passing away without having "taken care of business". The agent who helps them solve this riddle becomes the customer's hero.

Customers will ***sell themselves*** on your product, if their need is properly brought to the "light of day" and handled professionally by an expert agent.

I know this sounds obvious. Without a need for coverage being verbally reviewed by both the agent and customer alike, there will hardly be any appeal to the customer to move forward and pick a final expense plan for themselves. A final expense agent **must not assume** the need is there, then bypass talking about it. It must be *verbalized,* turned inside out. A customer is willing to discuss this with a skilled agent, who has done a good job of "warming up" the customer first.

I craft my words carefully at this point to emphasize my interest as a professional in the customer's lack of essential benefits.

This is a sample conversation between an agent and a customer to illustrate:

Agent: *Thank you, Mary, for sharing a little bit about yourself with me. I want to be sure that I am on the same page as you are, going in the same direction, ok?*

Client: OK.
Agent: *Mary, tell me what you feel your needs are. What were your thoughts and concerns **about your family** when you sent the card back in to me?*
(This is a MAJOR "tie down" question!)
Client: *When I saw the card, I thought I don't want my kids to have to pay anything on my funeral, like they did with Bill, my husband. I just want my own funeral to be cared for, so that nothing falls back on them.*
Agent: *OK, I think what I hear what you are saying, Mary is that you know your funeral will cost more than the $5,000 you already have in place. So, you just want a small, affordable plan that is permanent, never changes, pays out no matter what immediately to make up the difference. Is that what I hear you saying?*
Client: *Yes, That's right.*
Agent: *OK, Mary. I do feel comfortable moving forward with you, because you **care about your family**. You want to get something in place that will supplement your $5,000 coverage, because funeral costs go up 5% every year. And, you don't want your loved ones to have to dig into their own pockets to pay for your funeral or unplanned expenses. I'll do my best for you, and try to get all the extra no-cost benefits available there in* (client's city) *as well.*
Client: *Thank you.*
Agent: *OK. Let's move forward.*

    Again, it may go without saying, but I know too many agents who *do not verbalize* the customer's need back to them . Putting the customer's wishes into words by a skilled agent, assures the customer that their best interest is in the agent's care. It makes a customer feel their needs are validated, which adds value to the agent who understands them.
    This is so simple to do. Simply **repeat** what you hear the customer express. To the customer, it puts their needs to the forefront of the conversation. To the agent who masters this, a customer feels deep appreciation.

Sales are instantly made when there is mutual agreement. The customer's need is the best place to reach a common agreement.

I have often said that I make sales even before giving the customer a quote, even before premiums are known by the customer. How is that?

The sale is made when the customer buys YOU, the agent. If the customer buys into You, as a caring professional whose thoughts are for their best interest, the customer will want whatever you have to offer. The product is simply a benefit of knowing YOU.

Customer need is an area where trust is earned by an agent and buying decisions are made by the customer due to the customer's appreciation for putting their needs above all else.

Prequalify Customer: Health Questions

To add value to the benefits and to add respect to myself as a professional, I let the customer know beforehand my own expectations for their honesty while answering the health questions.

To set an official tone before reviewing the customer's health condition, here is a sample conversation between customer and agent to illustrate:

Agent: *Now, Mary, I do not require any physical exam or medical tests, but this is a state regulated program. As a Licensed Field Underwriter, I do ask a few basic health questions to be able to show you what benefits you qualify for, OK?*

Client: *OK.*

Agent: *We do a standard MIB check on health records with the Medical Information Bureau to verify your answers. This is just a standard check every Licensed Underwriter does to be able to put a life insurance policy in force. So, I'll tell you the same thing I tell everybody. Please, answer each question honestly and to the best of your knowledge, because we do a standard MIB check, OK?*

Client: *Sure. I've always been taught that honesty is the best policy.*
Agent: *Thank you.*

If the customer has a question about the Medical Information Bureau this is a good explanation for the customer.

The Medical Information Bureau is kinda' like the DMV where you get your driver's license. If there is anything on your driving record, the Division of Motor Vehicles has a record of it.

The Medical Information Bureau, Inc. is the same way. It is regulated under the federal Fair Credit Reporting Act and "HIPPA" Laws. It is a consumer reporting agency. Every time a person applies for life insurance, health conditions get reported to them. So, if you have anything on your health record, an insurance company can read it. We just do a standard check with the M.I.B. to verify your answers.

It is at this point I begin to inquire into the height and weight of the customer, their tobacco usage, and start a list of any serious physical challenges.

These health questions were covered in Chapter 1 under the section "The Product of Final Expense".

It is vitally important to accurately access the true picture of a customer's health. Before the actual health questions, I begin by asking the customer:

Agent: *Mary, before I ask the 8-10 Health Question here, go ahead and tell me anything I need to know about your health condition in the present and in the past. What is the **worst** thing about your health record? Go ahead and tell me the **worst** thing.*

This will guide the customer to get right to the point of the most potent physical challenges that may or may not qualify them for benefits. It allows the agent to get to the nitty-gritty of whether or not the customer qualifies without having to go through the entire list of prequalifying health questions.

This also makes the customer interactive and prompts the customer to be totally honest up front. It allows the customer to see that the agent is not wasting time on trivial health conditions. We are going right to the bottom-line of their health history.

After listing the customer's health information volunteered, I then ask the customer to list their prescriptions for me.

A customer may want to talk glowingly about their near perfect health, but when I ask what are you taking medicines for, the story may change. For instance, if a customer says, *"Oh yeah, well I just take a little pill for 'sugar'."* What the customer means to tell me is that they are a diabetic.

After the agent satisfies the inquiry for the worst things on the customer's health record, and a list of all prescriptions being currently taken, the agent should have a firm handle of the health condition of the customer. The 8-10 pre-qualifying health questions should be a breeze after that.

This is a sample conversation between agent and customer to illustrate:

Agent: *OK, Mary. Thank you for your honesty so far. We'll go through these 8 to 10 "Yes or No" Health Questions briefly together, ok?*
Client: *OK.*

Upon conclusion of answering all of the prequalifying health questions with the customer, I will prepare the customer for the free quote on their benefit plan. This is a sample conversation between agent and customer to illustrate:

Agent: *Thank you Mary. I do appreciate your honesty. This will let me know exactly what direction we can go in here. Now I know exactly which plan you qualify for. Would you please get a piece of paper and pencil ready, because we are going to write down some important things together, and I want to give you the direct number to my desk.*
Client: *OK. Give me a minute. I'll be right back.*

While the customer is getting ready their paper and pencil, I am writing down the name of their plan and the 3 options for the quote, which includes 3 coverage amounts and corresponding premium rates (Option 1, 2, & 3). A rate calculator instantly materializes the quote.

My full Sales Presentation Script MANUAL that thousands of agents utilize is all-inclusive to the exact verbiage that should be verbalized by an agent. I am leaving a lot of it out to only hit the highlights.

Sometimes a customer may have some serious physically debilitating condition(s) that have caused other insurance companies to refuse or disqualify the customer. If the customer lets me know of this disappointing experience, and if I know that I can qualify them, this creates an opportunity to console the customer in a way that adds value to myself, as their new insurance hero, and also adds tremendous value to the customer's situation:

Agent: *You do realize that if you went to a local insurance salesman there in* (client's city) *and told them that you want a free quote on life insurance, that you have diabetes, that you have high blood pressure, and that you have suffered a heart attack only 3 years ago, and you want immediate coverage from day one, do you know what the salesman would probably say?*
Client: *He would probably say "get lost".*
Agent: *Well, you might be right. He probably would not want to talk with you. Mary, let not your heart be troubled. This is the difference between talking to a Licensed Field Underwriter and just a regular salesperson. As long as I can see that you are following your physician's health plan, you are taking your medicines like you are supposed to, and you are living a healthy lifestyle, I don't have any problem pre-qualifying you for our top plan. I am not going to* **penalize** *you for your physical conditions. In fact, I am going to* **REWARD** *you for being a survivor. And, that's the way it ought to be. How does that make you feel?*
Client: *Thank you! It makes me feel great. I appreciate it.*
Agent: *You're welcome. Now, let's look at your plan.*

Interlude (Bank Account Verified)

Before I take the next step with a customer to share a free quote of their benefits as promised, it behooves me to take a moment and inquire about the existence of a bank account, or lack thereof.

It is rarely worth the time of an agent to stop the free-flowing, **paperless** telesales system, to then eat up hours with paperwork, paper applications, and payments sent through the mail. This is why the preferred payment method for premiums is automatic bank draft.

An agent is actually *losing* money by wrangling with paperwork, and paper applications, to get premium payments sent through the mail for the customer. By the time it takes an agent to accomplish getting all of this paperwork set up for a customer, the agent could have easily made more TELEsales, and instant commissions, via bank draft.

In addition, if a customer chooses a plan for themselves, and is determined to pay for it by payments through the mail, the 3-way underwriting Voice Application process between the customer and the insurance company may not be completed without the customer's bank account information anyway.

The "instant sale/instant commission" nature of telesales is best facilitated through a customer's ability to allow a monthly bank draft (Electronic Funds Transfer – EFT) to pay all premiums.

An agent's commission can be paid in the same week a policy is sold, if the customer's first premium is an immediate EFT. Typically, an insurance company can generate an agent's commission within 48 hours upon receiving the insured's initial premium by bank draft.

This is why all telesales agents are best suited to increase their own ability to handle any and all customer objections to an automatic bank draft.

Because it is the pride of telesales to offer "paperless" selling, we simply do not allow the customer to send a check or money order through the mail to pay premiums. Experience has taught us that policies may easily lapse, or require double payments, if a customer's premium payment gets lost or stolen in the mail.

It is in the best interest of both the customer as well as the agent to set up policy payments on a monthly bank draft, or bank service plan, from day one.

Suppose a client goes into the hospital years later, or worse, a nursing home. Their policy will not lapse if the bank is sending the premium payments to the insurance carrier automatically each month for the client.

Yet, if a client always sends in premium payments through the mail, a hospital or nursing home stay can stop the client's ability to mail payments, thus causing a lapse in coverage when the bill comes due, or a potential cancellation of the client's policy due to non payment. Years of coverage, as well as years of premium payments, are lost.

It is in light of these realities that an expert telesales agent needs to know if the customer has a bank account before sharing the benefits and free quote without "spooking" the customer in the process.

This proposes a challenge indeed for the agent to know that a customer, who may be interested in the benefits through a free quote, also has the ability to do an EFT through their bank, or not.

It is ideal for the agent to initially meet a customer over the telephone, make a sales presentation, sell a policy of the customer's choosing, complete a voice application, and get the policy issued, all in the same day (NOT weeks), all in 1-2 hours. The agent can then focus right back on the next lead prospect. This makes it possible for any telesales agent to sell one or more policies in the same day, while generating thousands of dollars of income commissions in a one week period, week after week after week.

Now, how does an agent verify a customer's bank account, or lack thereof? By letting the customer avoid a greater hassle, we offer them a lesser one.

Instead of doing a credit check on the customer, we simply want to be sure that they have not bounced any checks in last 15 days. If the customer answers *"No"*, we simply verify that they have an account in good standing. I take it one step further if I have established solid rapport with the customer at this point and ask if it is a checking or savings account.

(Exact, effective verbiage of a bank account inquiry is found in Dr. Clark's Sales Presentation Script MANUAL: **www.finalexpensesuccess.com/sales-script-manual**)

There is a reason why it is smart to ask if it is a checking or savings account. The only bank that is known to not draft out of a savings account is State Employee Credit Union, for the most part. Most all other banks and credit unions will allow an EFT through either a checking or savings account.

If a customer has a savings account through State Employee Credit Union, or does not have any bank account whatsoever, I simply go no further with the customer. A genuine explanation should be offered to the customer based on reasons to prevent the loss of coverage after years of payments explained in previous paragraphs.

In my own personal sales experience after a myriad of frustrating attempts, I have found that if an agent moves forward to give the free quote on benefits, then encourages the customer to later open a draftable bank account, to then rely on the customer to contact me when this task is completed, even if the customer picks a plan for themselves and **"promises"** to open a bank account immediately – IT NEVER HAPPENS.

Imagine that there are people who do not do what they say. Gasp!

I simply refuse to move forward with a customer who has no draftable bank account. The reasonable explanations I give to a customer without a bank account are the same reasons listed above in this section: 1) Checks & money orders get lost and stolen in the mail. People have to make double payments to catch up, or their policy lapses. 2) The insurance company will not complete the voice application without a customer's bank account. 3) Coverage is lost, if the customer goes into the hospital or nursing home for a lengthy stay. This typically stops payments that are normally sent through the mail.

Most of time, however, it is not a problem to verify that a customer has either a checking or savings account. By avoiding having to do a credit check, and by a customer's interest to what benefits they are entitled to, is usually all it takes for a customer to disclose initially the existence of a bank account.

Share Benefits

Thoroughly explaining the coverage benefits accomplishes several things.

This is where it gets interesting for the customer. Now, they will know exactly what the benefits are that they inquired about from the lead card they sent through the mail. The customer's interest is peaking at this point.

A skillful final expense phone sales agent will indirectly exercise the customer's peaking interest while curbing certain objections not yet mentioned.

In other words, an expert agent is going to kill two birds with the same stone (page) in the script. Not only will the customer receive the free quote, but I will also abolish one of the most lethal objections known to selling over the telephone.

It is at this point that I make sure the customer has paper and pencil ready and also inform the customer that I will walk them step by step through their qualified plan, because they need to know exactly what they are getting and how it works in favor of their family's future.

The deadliest objection that kills a sale is a customer's reluctance to make a buying decision today. Most avoid this decision by telling an unsuspecting agent that they need to "talk it over with _____".

However, if a customer decides to "talk it over with _____", instead of taking action on the opportunity before them, this "mystery person", who the customer wants to consult first before purchasing coverage, will typically advise **against** the customer taking the policy, because they have never met the agent who is selling the coverage.

Avoid this objectionary trap at the close by asking a simple question at this time:

Agent: *Mary, there is one question that I always ask at this point before I can share the benefits with you.*

AM I TALKING TO THE CORRECT PERSON?

Are you your own Financial Decision Maker, or do I need to have a son, a daughter, or a Power of Attorney on the phone with us? Is there anybody else who needs to be with you in this for you to make a decision?
Client: *No. I can make all of my own decisions.*

(I do not stop here. I go one step further!)

Agent: *So, Mary, if you see something that you want for yourself today, you can make this decision* **on your own** *,* **by yourself** *?*
Client: *Yes.*
Agent: *OK. I just wanted to be sure that I am speaking to the correct person.*

THIS MAY BE THE BEST SELLING TIP YOU WILL EVER READ IN BOOK FORM !!!!!!

It took countless, personal sales lost at the close due to this single objection, before I realized that I can head this one off at the pass, at this point in the Sales Script.

Pride alone in the customer being their own financial decision maker will vanquish any rhyme or reason later to delay a decision, so that the customer can "consult" someone else. A customer will have to flat out lie to the agent's face, if this objection is used by the customer at the close of the sale.

However, if the customer initially answers "Yes", that they do need someone else to be on the phone with them in order to make a decision, a wise agent will go no further with the customer and reschedule a later appointment when all financial decision making parties are on the phone together. Then, the expert agent will give the free quote on benefits.

After establishing that the customer can make a financial decision on their own, I volunteer the phone number that goes to my desk by saying to the customer, *"First things first. Let's write down my name and private phone line at the top of your paper."*

When my name and private phone number to my desk is written down by the customer, I always ask the customer to read it back to me. This ensures both the customer and agent that the customer can reach me direct.

It is then that I assure the customer that I will be their "contact representative for life". If they ever want a question answered, a beneficiary changed, or more coverage later, I can get that done quicker than anyone else at my department. I want my customer to know that they can pick up the phone, call straight to my desk, and talk to a real person.

It is imperative for the agent to offer a toll free 800 phone number to the customer. Saving a few pennies on a long distance call makes a huge difference in the mind of a customer. A toll free number is usually cost-free on an unlimited long distance calling plan, depending on the service provider. Typically, the only charge on a 800, 866, 877, or 888 phone line is if someone calls in on the toll free line and the agent picks up the phone to answer it. It then goes to the price per minute rate. Usually there is no cost to the agent for an incoming call on an 800 phone line, if the incoming call goes straight to voice mail. This is why I typically allow all incoming calls on my 800 phone line go directly to voicemail.

I constantly assure the customer throughout the quote delivery that every bit of information I share with them from this point forward will be in their "Welcome Packet" within 3-4 days and also in their actual policy within 10 business days.

Our insurance carriers send out issued policies directly to the customer within 10 business days. This saves an agent the postage of mailing it themselves several states away.

You'd be surprised what a small reminder like this does in the mind of a customer to "seal the sale" before the sale is actually made. Why? By allowing the customer to know when and what they will be receiving in the mail soon, the customer's apprehension over receiving nothing is alleviated.

Here, the customer is made aware that they do not have to write down every word that I say, only the most important things, which I will spell out for the customer. The customer is also assured that everything they hear in my free quote will be in writing and in their possession by virtue of the soon-coming "Welcome Packet" and actual policy within 10 business days.

I make sure the customer has their paper and pencil handy at this point to write down important numbers and the free quote on benefits they qualify for.

The name of the customer's plan, the name of the insurance company, the insurance company's history and financial solvency and website address, as well as state approval for the customer's plan of benefits are all spelled out here.

I have my own father insured by the plan that most of my customer's choose. I always share this fact with the customer who qualifies with the same company.

It is crucial to begin with the most important aspect of coverage explained first – Whole Life Insurance. This is not term insurance. Term means it will eventually *terminate*. This is why it is called *term*. It is *temporary coverage*. Term coverage typically runs out between ages 70-80.

I ask the customer to jot down the two most important words about their coverage plan – Whole Life. This means the coverage that they sign up for is the coverage that (beneficiary) gets within 48 hours to 5 business days. This is *permanent coverage*.

Because most of the people we serve final expense insurance to are on Disability or Social Security (a fixed income), they need a life insurance plan that is permanent, stays the same for life, and never runs out.

Final Expense Telesales (The New Way)

This is Whole Life insurance. They simply cannot afford rising premiums.

The payout of benefits will be paid 100% to (name of beneficiary). If the agent has not already done so, ask the customer who the benefits will be paid out to. Let the customer know that you want to refer to the correct person when you talk about the benefit payout.

A polite way for the agent to ask is, *"Mary who will I be working with in the future to pay out the cash benefits to (hopefully not any time soon)? Who do you trust to take of your funeral and final expenses? Who will be your primary beneficiary?"*

The full coverage amount will pay out normally within 48 hours to 5 days. The benefits are tax-free. It will not be touched by the government. It will also not go through state probate. I always emphasize this fact.

In explaining any additional no-cost benefits of the coverage, an expert agent will make a direct connection to the customer's lifestyle or situation. For example, if you are giving a quote to a farmer, place strong emphasis on the accidental death benefit where the policy coverage doubles in lieu of any accidental death caused by malfunctioning farm equipment or any farm-related accident.

Or, if the customer had a recent fall or accidental injury in their past, emphasize the accidental death benefit strongly. The coverage will double automatically if the customer's passing is caused by a fateful slip in the shower, tripping down a flight of stairs, or on a patch of ice.

It is vitally important for the customer to take ownership of their plan. A skillful agent will help the customer draw together the extra, no-cost benefits of the coverage to their own unique situation.

If the customer's adult children are out of work, or just struggling to "make ends meet", emphasize a plan's possible "Cash Draft" option. This will allow the beneficiary to go to *their local bank* and receive $1,000 immediately after the customer's passing, until the full claim is paid within 5 business days. This is great at a time like this when immediate financial necessities need to be taken care of, until the policy payout is sent in full to the beneficiary.

Just before we get to the free quote of 3 coverage amounts and corresponding premiums, I pivot to the monthly bank draft again briefly to allude to its importance. It is here that I give a definite yet brief emphasis that all plans are set up within security measures for seniors.

Instead of someone coming to their homes to collect payments – like they used to do in the old days - we just set up payments for you through your bank by **Automatic Deduction**.

"Automatic Deduction" is the key phrase I use to initially make the customer aware that the insurance company will be drafting their bank account for the premiums each month without actually saying "bank draft".

To use phrases such as – monthly bank draft, electronic fund transfer, and account draft plan – is to endanger the sale. Remember, the success of one sale is all in how it *sounds* to the customer. One wrong vibrating word can cause a customer to resist at the close.

I truthfully and simply let the customer know in palatable terms that their bank will "send in the payment" for them electronically each month by schedule on the day the customer chooses, the 1st through the 28th, because February has 28 days.

The customer's bank statement at the end of each month will reflect the same payment sent electronically to the same insurance company on the same day each month. The customer will always have a record of this payment in black-n-white in their bank statement each month, so they will always know what is going on.

If a customer balks at the idea of bank drafts at this point, it could be for several reasons:

> 1) The customer is used to sending payment through the mail.

Final Expense Telesales (The New Way)

2) The customer has a sour relationship with their local bank.
3) The customer may be overdrawn on their account.
4) The customer has an incorrect assumption about how bank drafts work.
5) The customer watched a segment on *20/20* the night before and was advised to never allow payments by bank draft.

An expert agent will remember that the underwriter phone interview with the customer (Voice Application) to be completed little bit later requires the bank information of the customer.

Upon listening to the customer's reason (whatever it is) for not wanting the bank to take care of their payment each month, here an appropriate response:

First of all, it's not like the insurance company reaches into your bank account with a "Big Hand" and takes out whatever they want each month. No No No No. That is NOT what happens. We would never want to do that. We would never be allowed to do that. What happens is, <u>your bank</u> will "send in" your premium payment for you electronically each month on the same day you choose is most comfortable for you.

My own father felt the same way as you do, (name of customer), when I qualified him for his permanent coverage here. However, when I explained 2 important advantages to my father for allowing his bank to send in his payment, he was then fine with it.

<u>2 Advantages to Monthly Bank Draft:</u>

1. One of the first things a family will do when someone passes is this. They will go to your bank to close out your account. At that point, the bank manager will bring out your bank statement. This is where your family will look at it and KNOW that no one has to dig into their own pockets to pay for your funeral. The bank will always have a record of your payments to the insurance company. We

expect you (the customer) to live another 20-40 years. By that time, you may forget you even have this coverage plan in your 90's, but the bank will **ALWAYS** have a record of it.

2. If you go into the hospital or a nursing care facility in the distance future, your bank will continue to keep your death benefits in place with premium payments remaining current. You could lose your final expense protection that you have paid on for years due to failure to send a payment through the mail. A Bank Service plan is normally no-cost and is for your best future interest, so you never lose your plan. You will always have a record each month of your exact payment in your monthly bank statement.

*You, (name of customer), will always have a record of your premium payments. Most importantly, banks always keep excellent records.

3. * OPTIONAL: (If the customer's Social Security check is direct deposited into their bank account) We do not allow payments through the mail for the same reason Social Security payments are deposited directly into your bank account. Checks and money orders get lost and stolen in the mail. After years of premium payments, one stolen payment through the mail can either lapse your policy or require you to make double payments to make up for a lost payment. A Bank Service Plan may avoid this threat to you each month. Besides, premiums are *lower* if you allow your bank to send in your payment for you each month. Would you prefer lower premiums or higher premiums?

From here, immediately pivot to the free quote, allowing the customer to know that these are the real numbers they have been waiting for, and everything else is academic, if they do not pick a plan for themselves.

I congratulate the customer for qualifying for the plan, while letting them know that the lowest premium rates are available right now in (customer's city), as well as all the additional no-cost benefits that I can insert into their plan today at no charge – ever.

Quotes

To begin the quote, I inform the customer that I will start low, as I give 3 options for them to look at. If the customer already has existing coverage in place, I will acknowledge this fact here, and refresh the memory of the customer that I will not be quoting a high coverage or premium amount.

A customer will appreciate a professional agent who has in mind a low cost when quoting premiums.
Example:

Agent: *Now, Mary, I am going to start low here when I give you the 3 options. You already have a $5,000 plan in place, so I am only going to quote a small coverage and low premium that would make up the difference for a decent, basic funeral, Ok?*
Client: *Ok. That sounds good.*
Agent: *Option #1 is $4,000 whole life coverage at ONLY $35 per month. That equals out to about $1.01 per day. Option # 2 is $5,000…..Option #3 is $6,000…….(the same verbiage as Option #1).*

(*Note: It is at this point some agents prefer to ask for the middle initial of the customer, and for beneficiary information by "assuming the sale". I do not. When a customer is making a life-changing, financial decision, I only want them to focus on one thing at a time. Why? It is my humble opinion that a customer does not want to feel "rushed" or distracted by an impetuous agent. When a customer is pondering a life choice, it may seem a little too presumptive to the customer, if an agent has their mind on something else, other than what the customer is focused on. The customer's middle initial and beneficiary information may easily be retrieved after the customer has chosen a plan for themselves. As a customer is focused on the quoted benefits, I want to "stay on the same page" as the customer, and focus on handling objections to seal the sale.)

Agent: *Now, Mary, I am going to stop with these 3 options for now. While you are looking at these 3, the $4,000 will double up to $8,000; the $5,000 up to $10,000; and the $6,000 will go up to $12,000 Total Coverage, in case of an accidental death. But, for a natural death, it would be the 4-5-or-$6,000 coverage. All three of these will pay out within 48 hours to 5 days after your passing. All three of these will begin immediately. There is no waiting period. The premiums never go up. The coverage never goes down. All three of these includes the no-cost...*(list extra benefits that come with the plan). *Now, Mary, you do qualify for up to $30,000 of coverage, but I started my quote low. Do you want to look at anything higher, or do you want me to stop right there?*

Client: *Just stop right there.*

Agent: *Ok. Now, if something, God forbid, were to happen to you tomorrow, how much coverage would pay out to* (name of beneficiary) *within 48 hours on the Option 1 Plan?*

Client: *$4,000.*

Agent: *You are correct. What if it is an accidental death, like if you trip and fall in the shower?*

Client: *Would it be $8,000 ?*

Agent: *Exactly right!*

(Repeat the same questions for Options 2-3).

Agent: *Now, Mary, do you like apple pie?*
Client: *Sure!*
Agent: *Well, if I baked you a delicious apple pie and gave it to you, you wouldn't have to eat the whole pie all at one time, would you?*
Client: *No.*

Agent: *Of course not. You can take a slice now that is comfortable for you. And, if you ever want another slice later, you can always come back to the apple pie and get another slice, correct?*
Client: Yes.
Agent: *Same thing is true here. You can take a slice of coverage now that is comfortable for you, and then if you ever want to get more coverage later, because funeral costs do go up 5% every year (you may want look at this again in another 3-5 years), you can come back later to ask for another slice of the "coverage pie". Does that make sense, Mary?*
Client: Yes.
Agent: *Once you are qualified, you are set for life! If you ever want more coverage later, you can check into more coverage by calling me direct.*

It is at this point that I place special emphasis that the customer does qualify for more expense plans, but in my professional opinion, these 3 Options cover what you (the customer) need now and will need in the future. I express my desire is to first of all make sure this plan is affordable and comfortable, while the premiums are low and the extra no-cost benefits are available. I ask for the sale by asking this question, "Now, Mary, which plan is the most comfortable for you on a monthly basis **right now**?"

"Right Now" are the very last words that I utter before closing my mouth to allow the customer to make a buying decision. I place deliberate emphasis on the phrase *"Right Now"*, because it lets the customer know that I am asking for their decision right now . Not next week. Not tomorrow. **Right Now**.

This is not an important decision tomorrow. This is an important decision today.

Now, silently allow the customer time they need to think and decide. After asking a customer to make a buying decision, there is an old selling cliché that goes: *"The first one to talk, loses."* This is a true statement.

Silence is at work on many different levels at this point in the sale. The first person (customer or agent) to break silence at this point is put immediately at risk of losing both leverage and control of the conversation. Why?

A customer usually needs a gentle "nudge" to make a buying decision today. A lot of times, silence at work can be the "mental nudge" needed (as the customer ponders this permanent protection for their family).

The first one to speak at the point of a buying decision is usually the one who ends up trying to convince the other one. This becomes a defensive position, especially if their preference is contrary to the other person's preference. It puts the person who spoke first automatically in a defensive position, and the other person in an upper-hand offensive position.

For the agent, a defensive position means not closing the sale today. For the customer, a defensive position means not being able to easily put off a buying decision.

I would rather a customer try to convince me why they can't make a buying decision today, than for me to have to convince a customer why they should not put off this decision to tomorrow. Anything could happen between today and tomorrow.

To maintain an upper-hand, offensive selling position I choose to remain tight-lipped while the customer either makes a buying decision or raises an objection. This keeps me on offense, ready to seal the sale!

The customer may also want clarification on a certain aspect of their coverage plan. Any question by the customer should be thoroughly answered by the agent. Then, it is CRUCIAL to bring the customer back to a point of decision by asking for the sale!

NEVER let the customer off the hook of making a decision. After an agent addresses anything that the customer needs clarification on, ALWAYS ask for the sale thereafter.

Here is a sample conversation between agent and customer to illustrate:

Agent: *Mary, which plan is more comfortable for you on a monthly basis,* **right now?**

Final Expense Telesales (The New Way)   111

(Moments of Silence)
Client: *Will the premiums ever go up?*
Agent: *No ma'am. Never. Even if your age or health changes later on, your premiums will never change.*
Client: *Ok…….Does my coverage start today?*
Agent: *Your coverage begins when the bank sends in your first payment for you on the day that is comfortable for you. We let you pick the day you want your coverage to start. Now, which one of these 3 options appeals to you the most?*
Client: *Well, the $6,000 coverage appeals to me the most, but I know that I can afford the $5,000 plan now. Can I call you tomorrow with my decision?*
Agent: *I am not allowed to "hold the benefits" open for anyone. I can promise you that your coverage quote is good for today. Now, if something should happen to you tonight, God forbid, which one of these plans would take care of your family?*
Client: *Do I have to make a decision today?*
Agent: *I prefer that we apply for the benefits, while you've got me on the phone with you. Take a moment to think about* (beneficiary) *receiving thousands of cash dollars within 48 hours after your passing for only $45 per month. What is that worth to you, as a cancer survivor? Remember, you can always call me directly for more coverage later, once I qualify you today.*
Client: *Will I get the policy for my family to look at?*
Agent: *Within 10 business days from today. Do you realize that your children and grandchildren will learn how to take care of their own final expenses when they will see your policy benefits in action?*
Client: *I guess you're right.*
Agent: *Which plan works best for your lifestyle and budget?*
Client: *Probably the $5,000 or $6,000 plan.*
Agent: *Mary, you are setting the right example before your family with the $5,000 plan. If you or your family want you to have more coverage later, you can let me know in the future by calling me direct. Is the $45 premium on the $5,000 plan or the $55 premium on the*

$6,000 plan going to fit best into your lifestyle and budget?
Client: *Probably the $45 plan for now.*
Agent: *Is the $5,000 plan the one you want?*
Client: *Yes.*
Agent: *Ok. I will circle the $5,000 plan at $45 per month on your application here....*

NOW is when I collect the customer's complete beneficiary information, middle initial, and bank account information, etc. I want the customer to be aware at this point that I am "filling out application information" to be utilized during the Voice Application later by saying:

Agent: *Remember, Mary, these benefits will be secured for you permanently. Your plan will start immediately, will never change, unless you want more later, and will pay out within 48 hours at your passing to* (name of beneficiary). *In just a moment, my assistant will come on the line with us to complete your 5-10 minute Voice Application to make sure I have everything spelled right, and we have your plan set up just the way you want it. Now, Mary, what is your middle initial.....*

Exact, entire sales verbiage that phone sales agents utilize to close a sale is available at:
www.finalexpensesuccess.com/sales-script-manual

Close The Sale, Customer Objections

Dr. Clark's complete Agent Rebuttal / Customer Objection Script:
www.finalexpensesuccess.com/objection-rebuttal-sales-script

Any customer objection to making a buying decision today can be slight apprehension over a minor unaddressed detail, or a polite way of saying "not right now".

Rarely does any customer ever bluntly say "No, I do not want your coverage". Simply put, a customer *objection* is not always a *rejection*. It is simply the customer's way of telling me **how to make a sale**.

Remember, the Big Purchase decision by the customer at the close is made up of previous smaller decisions ("tie downs") with the customer throughout the sales script.

I look at customer objections at the close as a final plea for help with a certain obstacle in the customer's way to being able to purchase coverage today. It is the final "tie down".

The customer is giving me their objection, because they want me to know that they need my help to overcome something specific without actually saying so.

An expert telesales agent has already curbed several *potential* objections previously in prior pages of the sales script, before these even have a chance to surface at the close, such as: 1) I need to consult with ____, before I make my decision. 2) I do not have a bank account. 3) I want this quote sent to me in the mail before making a decision. 4) My poor health makes it impossible for me to qualify. 5) I did not send any card in to your department. 6) I was only checking into benefits for someone else. 7) I have no need for this coverage, or I already have enough coverage. 8) I do not have a steady source of income to afford your plan.

ALL of these potentially hazardous objections at the close of a sale are previously neutered in the Sales Presentation Script by a skillful telesales agent. Therefore, these objections become null and void, or virtually nonexistent, at the close.

There are only 1-4 main objections at this point that an expert agent will hear, if the sales script was thoroughly and previously followed. They are:

- ❖ I want more time to think about it.
- ❖ I refuse to give my personal information (Social Security number or bank account information) over the phone to someone I do not know.
- ❖ This seems like not enough coverage for the premium payment.
- ❖ I can put the premium payments in the bank and save up to pay for my own funeral.

After spending at least 30 minutes to 1½ hours on the telephone getting to know a customer, prequalifying their health condition, giving a free quote, and helping a customer choose a plan that is best suited for their family situation, a professional telesales agent deserves a straight answer from the customer for the agent's time.

Because an expert agent talks to literally scores of people every day who have previously inquired into end-of-life benefits, a customer does not realize that the longer they put off the opportunity for immediate coverage, the greater they are at risk of **losing** coverage due to changes in their health, unpredictable changes in coverage premiums, and an agent's loss to forget a procrastinating customer.

It behooves the expert agent to give the customer a gentle "nudge" to decide today if this coverage is right for them. If the customer has inadequate or no coverage at all for funeral and burial expenses, and can also afford the monthly premiums, the agent would ultimately be doing a disservice to the customer's family to not try to close the sale immediately.

I simply do not play games with a customer at the close. It's either yes or no. Is this coverage right for you, or not. Let us be honest with one another. An agent's time is really money, when you are self employed. So, I expect nothing less than a straight answer from the customer. I have no time for any cat-n-mouse games.

I accept the challenge of objections head-on for what the customer says. However, I want to get to the bottom of any customer objection to know if it is based upon a need for my professional assistance to overcome a real obstacle in the life of a customer, or is the customer simply saying "no" to my coverage plan altogether. I need to know which it is. Is this a real sale, or not?

"I need more time to think about it"

The most common customer objection in my 10 years of experience as a National Top Producer of final expense life insurance is the ole' "I need to think about it" routine.

"Really?", is my first reaction to the customer.

Final Expense Telesales (The New Way)　　　　　115

This surprises me as the customer has already clearly given to me several, well defined, buying signals throughout the sales script. I NEVER move forward with a customer, unless I know for sure that I have a buyer on the telephone within the first 10 minutes of the initial conversation.

Each page of the script ties down small confirmations from the customer to keep moving forward. I, as a professional life insurance expert, would never be at the point of closing a sale, unless the customer previously made it crystal clear that they desire my assistance <u>today</u> with coverage.

I <u>always</u> assume the customer wants to think about it **while I am on the phone with them**.

If a customer then says, "No, I meant can I call you back tomorrow and tell you my answer?" My reply is something that may astound you. It is a very simple reply. Yet, 98% of all final expense agents are too afraid to put this verbiage into practice.

Simply say NO.

Here is a sample conversation between a customer and agent to illustrate:

Agent: *Mary, which plan is most comfortable for you on a monthly basis **right now**?*
Client: *I need some time to think about it.*
Agent: *Really? Ok, I'll give you some time to make your decision while I am working here at my desk. Just let me know when you are ready.*

(*Note: Sometimes this is all it takes for the customer to spend a few moments to make a decision. After a few moments of silence, they are ready to let me know of their choice. If not...)

Client: *I meant can I call you back tomorrow after I have made my decision?*
Agent: *No ma'am, I prefer that we apply for the benefits you want, while you've got me on the phone with you.*

*Note: I, as an experienced agent, already realize that **99%** out of *thousands* of people who say they will call me back after receiving a free quote NEVER CALL ME BACK. There are many reasons for this on the customer's side: 1) The free quote shared later with a family member or trusted friend will always advise against doing business over the telephone, simply because *they have never spoken with me, the agent*. To the person giving advice to the customer, I am just a stranger, not a professional. 2) TV or mail advertisements can easily confuse and frustrate a deciding customer, thus causing them to "just forget the whole thing". 3) Time works against both customer and agent to be able to get the coverage as random changes in life occur.

It is for these reasons that I will not let the customer off the hook loosely, if they truly want coverage that I have spent my valuable time processing for them. Whether the customer understands or not, I need to know if they are a real buyer. The customer's need for coverage was previously addressed by the customer. The customer has already stated that they are their own financial decision maker. The customer has also confirmed that they can afford the plan and have means to pay for it.

Any customer on a fixed income (Social Security or Disability) **already knows** that they get paid the very same amount each month. They work with the same budget every month and know what they can and cannot afford. By an agent saying "no" to a customer, it gently jolts them back into an immediate buying decision. If they truly want the coverage, they will understand and respond accordingly. If they refuse, or change their disposition negatively towards me, then I know the customer is not being completely honest about really needing my help today.

An agent will feel a large "lump in the throat" by saying "no" to a customer. Your heart may even sink down to your feet. Consider this. What do you have to lose? The customer is already backing out by asking for more time to "think about it". An agent has MORE to lose by letting the customer off the hook, and not holding them accountable to a previous confirmation that the customer indicated earlier in the sales script that they need professional assistance with coverage today. A customer rarely hears an insurance person tell them no. It takes control away from the customer and lends power over the conversation to the agent at the close. A simple "no" sets an expert agent apart from practically any other professional agent that the customer may have previously dealt with. Because an agent knows what he wants from the customer (a straight answer either way), it actually generates *respect* for the agent. Sales are made based on if the customer respects the agent, and **not** necessarily if the customer likes the agent. Although I enjoy being liked, I would much rather be *respected* by the customer. This is key to becoming a good closer. Don't be shy. Simply say No.

Client: *You mean I can't have time to think about this before I make my mind up?*
Agent: *Absolutely! Take all time you need. As I am working at my desk, just let me know when you have made your mind up to the plan that works best for you.*
Client: *Can't I think about think overnight and get back with you a few days from now?*
Agent: *Oh my, no ma'am. If you are serious about this permanent protection on you for your family, I do not need any money today, but I do prefer to qualify you for the one that you want. I prefer that you decide which one is right for you, while you've got me on the phone with you.*
Client: *Can you call me back in a day or two and then I will tell you which plan I want?*
Agent: *Mary, no ma'am. This is not important tomorrow. This is important today. You can wait another 68 years, if you want to. Makes no difference to my pay grade. However, you have to go through me in order to qualify for the state approved benefits here. I prefer that we apply for the benefits, while you have me on the phone with you. Now, which of these 3 plans appeal the most to you?*

Client: *You mean you want me to decide today which plan I want?*
Agent: *Yes ma'am. Take your time. I want to be sure that this is affordable for your lifestyle and budget. I'll give you a few moments to decide.*
Client: *Ok.........I think I'll start with the $5,000 plan.*

"I do not share bank account information"

This smokescreen objection is unfounded by most customers who use it. Truth is, if a customer writes checks to pay bills, their personal bank account information is at the bottom of each check that they hand over to the pizza delivery guy, or grocery store clerk, whom the customer does not know from Adam.

If the customer's Social Security check is direct deposited into their bank account (it is ok for the agent to ask this of the customer if solid rapport has been built with the customer throughout the sales script), it is simply their local bank applying the same principle by sending a payment electronically to the insurance company's account. It is an electronic transfer of funds – all of which are recorded on paper for the customer on their monthly bank statement.

As stated previously in this book, it is in the best interest of both the customer as well as the agent to set up policy payments on a monthly bank draft, or bank service plan, from day one. A hospital stay or weeks on vacation can potentially end a policy when failure to make a payment through the mail puts a policy the customer has paid on for years in immediate peril. Also, lost or stolen payments in mail may require the customer to make double payments to keep a policy in force.

It is for these reasons that an expert telesales agent must "nudge" the customer respectfully to allow premiums to be paid through the bank. This means an agent must secure the customer's bank account information.

An expert telesales agent builds trust in a specific way before verifying bank account information with the customer. Thanks to a highly effective sales technique, we are able to verify some of the customer's bank information at **www.gregthatcher.com.**

It greatly increases credibility with a customer when an agent has the ability to verify certain bank information, before the customer voluntarily discloses the full bank information required to set up a monthly bank draft for premium payments.

However, a few customers may balk at sharing their account information over the telephone with an agent. An agent must be firm, unwavering in this resolve to be able to qualify the customer for their benefits TODAY. Whether the customer agrees or not, an expert agent is doing them a tremendous favor by setting up their plan payments securely through their local bank.

The bank will always have a record of payments. The customer will also have a record of payments in their bank statement each month. A grieving family closing the bank account of the dearly departed will recognize these premium payments to a life insurance policy. Even if the policy has been in force for decades, and the customer may have been senile for years, the bank will always have a record of payments to keep those in charge of burial costs informed. This is a tremendous benefit for the customer's family when the funeral home has their hand stuck straight out during the worst week of a grieving family's life. It lets the family know that no one has to dig into their own pockets to cover funeral costs.

If a customer has had a previously poor experience with a bank, a wise agent will listen intently to the complaint. Since the agent is hearing only one side of the story, it is best for the agent to first apologize for the poor experience (I'm sorry this happened to you). Then, simply assure the customer that our department has great relations with (name of customer's bank). Federally insured banks have never missed a payment, unless there were not enough funds in the account to make a payment. Otherwise, everything is going to be fine.

Here is a sample conversation between a customer and agent to illustrate rebuttals to this particular objection:

Agent: *Ok, Mary, you said that you have not bounced any checks. Are you with a bank or a credit union?*
Client: *A bank.*
Agent: *What is the name of your bank?*
Client: *Bank of America.*
Agent: *Are they local for you, there, in Pineville?*
Client: *No, we go to the one in New Berry.*
Agent: *Ok. Mary I am going to verify the routing number with you for Bank of America in New Berry. If you have your checkbook handy, I am going to read these number to you. I need to make sure you have the correct routing numbers on your check, ok? So, get your checkbook in front of you please, so we can verify the numbers together.*
Client: *Ok, just a minute. I need to go get my checkbook.*
Agent: *I'll get some things ready for you here at my desk, while you are doing that. Go right ahead.*
(Agent looks up the bank routing number at: **www.gregthatcher.com, or Google: Bank name, what is routing number**).

Client: *Ok, I am back now.*
Agent: *Mary, if you look at the bottom left corner of your check, you should see a line of numbers. The first nine digits is called your Routing Number. I am going to read the routing number for Bank of America to you. Make sure our numbers match, ok? They are as follows, beginning at the bottom left corner – 123456789. Is this correct?*
Client: *Yes. That is correct.*
Agent: *Now, read to me the numbers after that.*
Client: *Aren't these number my account numbers?*
Agent: *Yes ma'am, they are, Mary.*
Client: *I don't give out my bank numbers over the phone. I watched 20/20 last night, and they said never give your bank information to anyone. Can't I just send in my payments through the mail?*

Agent: *I appreciate and understand your concern, Mary. Is your Social Security check direct deposited into your bank account each month?*
Client: *Yes.*
Agent: *Do know why Social Security does it that way now? Because, checks get lost or stolen through the mail. Your plan is set up for security reasons on a bank service plan to prevent this from happening. Just like Social Security, the insurance companies have trouble with payments being stolen or lost in the mail as well. You never want your policy to lapse or terminate, because a payment did not make it to the insurance company. You could potentially lose protection coverage that you have paying on for years. Does that make sense to you?*
Client: *How will I know the bank is doing it right?*
Agent: *Great question! There are 2 advantages to allowing your bank to send in your payments:*

> *1) You will always have a record of your payment each month in your bank statement that Bank of America sends to you monthly. I bank with Sun Trust, and I have my payments set up on the 15$_{th}$ each month. When I receive my bank statement from Sun Trust at the end of the month, I always have a record of it, where I can see that Sun Trust sent in the same amount to the same company on the same day every month by schedule. You will see the same thing on your bank statement from Bank of America. You will always have a record of it.*
>
> *2) The second advantage is this. Mary, one of the first things your family will do when someone passes away is go to the bank to close your account. At that point the bank manager will bring out your bank statement. This is where you family will look at it and know that your financial burden will not fall back on them. The bank will always have a record of it, You will also have a record of it each month. It is just safe for everyone, because you can trust your bank, right?*

Client: Yes. I suppose. I just don't feel comfortable giving my bank account number to anyone.
Agent: Mary, have you ever written a check and paid for items at a grocery store or Wal-Mart?
Client: Yes.
Agent: Your account number is at the bottom of every check that you hand over to a store clerk whom you do not know. Ever paid a pizza delivery guy with a check?
Client: A few times.
Agent: It is the same information at the bottom of your check that we require to process your application here over a secure line. Your information will not be shared with anyone else. There is no funny business going on here. We have never had a problem with anyone's account at the Final Expense Department.
Client: Are you sure you can't just send me a bill and let me pay with a check in the mail?
Agent: I understand, Mary. Suppose you pulled your vehicle into a convenience store gas station to fill up with gas. On the gas pump you notice a make-shift sign that reads "No Personal Checks". Would you be the type of person that would fill up your vehicle with gas, knowing what the sign says, then walk in to pay and insist on using a personal check, because you don't care what the sign at the pump reads? We simply do not allow personal checks through the mail, for your protection.
Client: I see your point.
Agent: Besides, Mary, premium payments are higher when paid through the mail, if we allowed it, because of administrative costs. Let's move forward. Let's get the lowest premiums. Let's put this last piece of the puzzle together, then you are set for life with coverage. I am going to read your routing number starting at the bottom left corner, 123456789. Now read the numbers right after that, Mary.
Client: 748257703....

Final Expense Telesales (The New Way)

I do not share my Social Security number.

A customer who desires to qualify for final expense protection today will normally follow the given procedures of "filling out an application" over the phone. THIS IS KEY VERBIAGE (fill out application).

After a customer chooses a plan for themselves, let them know that you are going to complete their application with them. Why? Because everyone basically knows that if you fill out any kind of application for anything, it is going to require a space for the Social Security number.

I usually ask for the Social Security number last after all contact, beneficiary, physician, and bank information has been verified. By this time, the customer is into the ebb and flow of volunteering applicatory information. The Social Security number at this point becomes part and parcel to the normal process.

Here is a sample conversation between agent and customer to illustrate the Social Security number objection and effective rebuttals:

Agent: *Ok, Mary, thank you for your honesty on the application here so far. The last bit of information on your application makes this an accurate document. What is your "Social"* (Social Security number).

(*Note: The single word 'Social' sounds more inviting and relaxed than 'Social Security number'. It is a subtle yet huge difference, so that the agent does not spook the customer at this point.)

Client: *I don't want to give my Social Security number over the telephone.*
Agent: *I understand Mary. I appreciate your concern. If you were sitting across from my desk applying for life insurance, you would fill out your Social Security number to put down on a paper application for life insurance, right?*
Client: *I suppose so.*
Agent: *You realize that any legally accurate document requires a Social Security number, correct?*
Client: *Yes.*

Agent: *Well, I am simply filling out your application here for you. This number will not be passed around. It is kept confidential. You are speaking on my private and secure phone line now.*
*Mary, this is a legally accurate document. We need to verify your identity, so the benefits will go to the right person - (beneficiary name). We need to know that you are you. Again, this is a **legal transaction**. All information must be kept true and confidential. Your benefits will not be processed without verifying your identity. This is the last bit of information on your application. So, go ahead, what is your social?*
Client: *Are you sure I have to give you my Social Security number?*
Agent: *Yes ma'am. I may not put the benefits into place without it. This is an accurate, legal document that entitles you to your benefits. We have never had one complaint about trouble with Social Security numbers at my department here. This is confidential information on your application simply submitted to the insurance carrier for proper processing. I am trusting you to give the correct information. Now, what is your social?*
Client: *Ok. It is 256.....*

This seems like not enough coverage for the premium payment

Because it typically has been years ago, even decades, since the customer took out any life insurance coverage on themselves, they somehow expect the premium rates and coverage amounts to magically be the same today.

It is the expert agent who will reeducate the customer, in terms they can understand, that the customer is not as young or healthy as they once were 20 years ago, limiting their insurance choices, and causing premiums to be higher at this time.

Here is a sample conversation between customer and agent to illustrate this objection and effective rebuttal:

Client: *You know, $6,000 just does not seem like enough coverage for the premium payment of $50 per month.*
Agent: *I understand, Mary. You are 68 years young now. How many years ago did you take out your $4,000 coverage that you have already in place?*
Client: *Oh my goodness, it's been about 15 years ago.*
Agent: *The reason why I am asking, Mary, will give you a clearer picture of your insurance options at this point in your life, Ok?*
Client: *Ok.*
Agent: *There are two things in insurance that determine the coverage and premiums you can get. Do you know what they are?*
Client: *Not really.*
Agent: *It is your age and your health.*
Now, Mary, I don't about where you come from, but where I come from, people do not get any younger. Would you agree?
Client: *That's right.*
Agent: *And, the more we age, do we get healthier or more unhealthy?*
Client: *Unhealthy.*
Agent: *You're right. Now, Mary, even though you have a heart condition, I am still willing to qualify you at my department, whereas a lot of insurance companies would not want to even talk to you.*
Now, if you went to the doctor tomorrow, and he put you on insulin, your premiums for this same coverage would be $75 per month for $6,000 whole life coverage, instead of $50 per month.
These premiums will never get any cheaper than they are right now. Mary, you have the Top Plan in front of you that you qualify for with me. I will be your personal contact representative for life. You can always pick up the phone and talk to me, if your family wants to pay for more coverage on you later. Which one of the 3 options will take care of your family, if something were to happen to you tonight?
Client: *It would be the $6,000 plan.*

I can put these payments into my bank and save up for my own funeral.

I must say it is comical and amazing how a 72 year old senior receives this financial strategy revelation now of saving up for a funeral, while talking with me on the phone. It never occurred to them for 72 years, until now?

Of course, it is too risky for a senior over age 65 to begin a 20 year savings plan living on a fixed income. Truthfully, those over 70 years, especially, are living on "bonus time".

A professional telesales agent realizes that time and savings options are stacked against a senior 65 and above. It would be foolhardy to assume a senior at this age living on Social Security can save enough money for a $7-12,000 funeral who has not already done so by now.

On the other hand, it would be wise to redirect the thinking of a senior customer, who desires to pay for their own funeral, into a final expense coverage plan.

Here is a sample conversation between customer and agent to illustrate this objection and effective rebuttal:

Client: *You know, I can just put this $50 a month into a savings account for 10 years and have $6,000 to pay for my funeral, plus interest! Why do I need your $6,000 coverage if I can do that?*
Agent: *I understand, Mary. However, you are missing the most important point to all of this.*
Client: *What's that?*
Agent: *Mary, do you have a personal banker, there at Bank of America? You know, someone you would go to if you needed a loan. Maybe the banker who secured your mortgage or car loan. Do you have a personal banker at your local bank that you like to deal with?*
Client: *Yes.*
Agent: *Ok. What is the first name of your personal banker?*
Client: *Marty.*
Agent: *Ok. Marty. Perfect.*

What if you went to see Marty there at Bank of America, there in (city). And, you told Marty that you were going to put $50 into the bank every month. In return for your $50 deposit per month into Marty's Bank of America, you want the bank to give your family $6,000 when you die. Even if you pass away next month, you want Marty and Bank of America to give to your family $6,000 cash immediately, because of your $50 deposit each month. Would they do it?
Client: *No.*
Agent: *Of course not. Mary, you are getting $6,000 permanent protection for only $50 per month. When you make your first premium payment,* **your funeral is largely paid for.** *Even if you pass away next month your funeral is largely paid for. Now, which one of these 3 options appeals the most to you? Which one would take care of your family, if something were to happen to you tonight?*
Client: *But if I pay in $50 every month for 10 years, I will pay in more than $6,000.*
Agent: *I understand. Mary, let not your heart be troubled. You will never pay in more than the coverage amount of your policy, if you do not want to. Here's why.*
2 Reasons:
   1) The Mortality Rate. The female life expectancy average is 78 years. You are 72 now. In 6 years, you will have to outlive 99% of all females your age to pay your premiums for 10 years to equal $6,000. And, we hope that you do! Point is, these premium payments are based on the Mortality Rate, so that you do not lose money, or outlive your policy. Secondly...
   2) Let's suppose you outlive the female expectancy of 78 years and live to be 100. Typically, the insurance company notifies a customer when a plan "matures' at age 100. At this point you generally have 2 options: a) be paid your cash value that has accumulated inside of your policy, Or, b) you may be able to keep your coverage as a paid-up policy. You are rewarded for being a

survivor and will not lose your coverage, or premiums that you paid in.

The point is Mary, in order for something to legally be called insurance, by state law, there must be a **risk on both parts**. There must be a risk on the insurance company. And, there must be a risk for the client. Now, there is no more risk to the insurance company when you pay in as much as the coverage amount, so you are provided with a couple options at the point a policy "matures". You will never pay in MORE than the coverage amount is worth, if you do not want to, ok?
Client: Ok.
Agent: Now, which one of these 3 plans appeals to you the most?
Client: It would be the $6,000 plan....

Voice Application

Once the customer has settled on a particular plan of coverage that is comfortable for them, I begin to "fill out the application" with the customer.

Actually I am continuing to jot down the customer's information on the printed out lead that I have been taking notes on the whole time to be submitted later on an online electronic application. This information will be required for the underwriter interview in a few moments.

After securing beneficiary information, bank account information, dates of the customer's first payment and subsequent monthly payments, Social Security number, and all other important application information on my checklist, I will then prep the customer on the underwriter interview to complete the process.

I want the customer to be prepared and know exactly what to expect when the insurance company underwriter is on the phone with the customer in a few moments asking the customer questions.

Let the customer know that after the 5-10 minute Voice Application is completed, they should remain on the line for the agent to offer a parting gift and give congratulations.

Final Expense Telesales (The New Way) 129

Listed below is a checklist of common questions that both the agent and the customer will be asked during the 3-Way Call with the insurance company underwriter. This list varies depending on the insurance carrier.

Agent Will Be Asked

> Agent Writing Number (Appointment number with the insurance company).
> Agent phone number.
> Agent permission to complete the Voice Application with a Voice Signature.
> Agent state calling from.
> State in which the client is calling from.
> Client name and contact information.
> Client state of birth.
> Client occupation. ("Retired", if on Social Security, or Disability).
> Client beneficiary information.
> Client bank account information and monthly draft date.
> Client primary physician.
> The name of the plan and premium amount the client is applying for.
> Is the client replacing existing coverage?
> Did you read the 4 Disclosure statements to the client?

Customer Will Be Asked

> Permission to complete the Voice Application with a Voice Signature.
> Contact information.
> Date of birth.
> Are you a U.S. Citizen?
> State born in.
> Social Security number.
> Plan name and monthly premium amount.
> Beneficiary Information.
> Physical reason for Disability payments.

Medical Questions. (Same health questions previously asked by the agent.).
Is this policy going to replace your existing coverage?
Verify bank account information and draft date of premiums.
Do you want the no-cost Automatic Premium Loan Option? (Cash value pays premiums in an emergency)
Compliance Acknowledgement (Did your agent read the 4 Disclosure Statements to you?).

There is specific verbiage that an agent must use when the 3 way call with a customer is placed into the insurance company underwriting department to be allowed to do a Voice Application over the telephone. This exact verbiage makes the underwriter immediately aware that an authorized agent has a customer on the phone now ready to complete a Voice Application.

Not just any agent "off the street" can be allowed to complete a Voice Application. Final expense phone sales is *exclusive* with certain insurance carriers. The correct verbiage to complete a Voice Application is shared with qualified and approved agents:
www.finalexpensesuccess.com/total-sales-success-kit.

The insurance company's underwriting departments that we work with makes special allowances for deaf customers, as well as foreign language customers to complete the Voice Application.

As long as the insured is on the telephone, the underwriter can typically speak through an interpreter on the customer's end. I have personally insured customers with these unique hearing or language challenges on our selling platform in this fashion. It normally works very smooth and comfortable for all parties involved.

A professional telesales agent will make the underwriter aware beforehand of these unique situations.

Here is a sample conversation between customer and agent to illustrate the pivot into the Voice Application:

Agent: *Ok, Mary. One last thing we will do together to secure your rates and all the no-cost benefits to your plan is this. One of my Underwriting Technicians will join us on the call to verify your information over a secure line, and complete your application, so no one will have to come out to visit you. I can't activate your plan today, but I do need to secure your coverage benefits permanently for you and your family. The way I am going to do this for your security is right here over the phone. To make this a Legal Document, I will ask my assistant to come on the phone with us on a secure line to verify all your information on the application, and to make sure that I have everything spelled right, ok?*

Client: *Ok.*

Agent: *Then, she will ask you the very same health questions that I have gone over with you just to verify your answers one last time. I'll then submit your application to the Final Department. They will approve it. Then, you are set for life! You'll never have to think about this again the rest of your life. It goes with you the whole way, never changes, and will pay out within 48 hours at that time.*

Client: *Sounds great.*

Agent: *That's because it is great. Now, stay on the line after my assistant is finished, so that I can congratulate you and let you know about our parting gift, ok?*

Client: *Ok.*

Agent: *One last thing, Mary. I almost forgot. At the very end, my assistant will ask you if I read the 4 Disclosure Statements to you. If you were sitting across from my desk, signing a paper application, I would have you read these on the application. They are as follows:*

> *1) Medical Information Bureau Notice. This is a standard MIB check that I have already informed you about. Every licensed underwriter does a standard check on health records to verify your*

answers to the health questions to be able to put a life insurance policy in force.
2) Authorization to Obtain and Disclose Information. This means that a licensed underwriter reserves the right to contact any hospital, health clinic, or medical institution, if need be, about your health.
3) Notice of Information Practices. This means that (customer first and last name), *or your representative, has a right to receive a copy of any information collected on your health or background.*
4) Fraud Warning. This means that any person who knowingly commits false statements on an application can be guilty of an offense, but that we have completed the application full and true to the best of our knowledge and belief.

Mary, these are the 4 Disclosure Statements. My assistant will ask you if I read them to you. Please answer accordingly.

Now, Mary, do you have any final questions before I bring my assistant on the phone with us to complete our 5-10 minute Voice Application?

Client: *No.*

Agent: *Ok, you stay right there. I am going to see who is working today. It'll probably be Trish or Vanessa. I'll bring her on the line with us in just a moment. I'll be right back, ok?*

Client: *Ok.*

(*Note: The agent puts the customer on "hold". The agent places a 3-Way call to the insurance company underwriting department. Once the underwriter is on the 2nd phone line, the agent patches all 3 phone lines together to complete the phone interview.)

Referrals

Dr. Clark's complete Collecting Referrals Sales Script:
www.finalexpensesuccess.com/referral-sales-script

Upon conclusion of the phone interview between and the insurance company underwriter and the insured, the phone conversation is brought back to both the agent and the newly insured client.

The wise agent should make a big deal out of congratulating the client. Next, the agent will seal the sale by sharing information about the Welcome Packet being sent immediately to the client. Finally, the agent will ask for referrals from the client without sounding like asking for referrals.

Further seal the sale by reinforcing the client's commitment to their plan of coverage, as well as how to address any potential negative feedback from the client's family members who "poo-poo" the client's decision to purchase coverage.

Here is a sample conversation between client and agent to illustrate:

*Note: We pick up the conversation after the underwriter has hung up their line on the 3-way call.

Agent: *Ok, Mary, Let me be the first to say "Congratulations"!!*
Client: *Thank you. I hope I did ok in the interview.*
Agent: *You were perfect. May I be the first to say again, "Congratulations". I feel honored to be your personal contact representative for life. Thank you for the privilege of allowing me to serve your family.*
Client: *You're welcome. Thank you for helping me to get this coverage in place. It is something I have been meaning to do, since my husband died 2 years ago.*
Agent: *Mary, I am not going to forget about you, either. I'll be checking in with you from time to time. Now,* **do you feel good** *about the decision you made today?*
Client: *Yes, I do.*
Agent: *What my company and I are doing is making a commitment to you and your family. I take a lot of pride in watching these cash benefits pay out within 48 hours, but it also requires a commitment from you to have the money available for your bank to make the monthly payment. If you have any trouble financially, or if you want more coverage, will you call me?*
Client: *I sure will.*

Agent: *Mary, my secretary will send you your Welcome Packet in the mail today. Inside will be my business card, a letter from me, and a Memorial Guide. This is a professional booklet for you to record all of your final wishes, important legal or financial information, funeral arrangements, and any last words of love you wish to record for your family. This is our gift to you. Then, your actually policy will arrive in the mail within 10 business days.*

Client: *Sounds good. I appreciate it so much.*

Agent: *Mary, a lot of times when family members learn about your plan for coverage, you may share the information as a positive benefit to them, but they may unfortunately take it as a negative. Sometimes, children especially will say, "Mom, you should not have done that. We'll take care of your funeral cost. Just go ahead and cancel your policy." What they really mean, Mary, is that they do not want to think about their mother dying. So, what you have to do is stay strong and stick to your plan. Remember, you are setting the right example before your entire family that will show your children and your grandchildren how to take care of their own financial burden that everyone leaves behind. They will learn how to do this the right way from you. So, stick to your plan, Ok?*

Client: *Ok.*

Agent: *Now, Mary, before I let you get back to enjoying your day, the truly unique thing about this program is that you have the ability to sponsor unlimited family and friends. You can provide the same benefits you qualify for to your family and friends without them having to send a card in. Who would you like to share these benefits with? I will give them a quote without charging them one penny. Can you think of someone who might have a need for this? I can put them into my system under your name in case they call in.*

Client: *Probably my brother, Bill....*

(*Note: The agent writes down the age and contact information of all referrals given by the client.)

Agent: *Mary, I'll keep these names in my system that you have sponsored. You call them first.* Let them know about the plan you were able to qualify for, and let them know that they may also qualify. *I will not call anyone, until you have called first, Ok?*
Client: Ok. I am going to call my brother right now. I'll let you know if he is interested.
Agent: *Thank you, Mary. I will wait for a couple days or a week before I call Bill, unless I hear from you sooner.*

The very last thing I say to a client before hanging up the telephone is *"Take Care"*. I want the last word my client hears from me to be the word "care", because I do care about each client, each family protected, each sale.

* Referral Call Script:

Hi there (name of referral). *This is* (name of agent) *at the Final Expense Department. My client,* (name of the client), *received benefits that you may be privileged to as well, because she sponsored you. This is a state approved plan with additional no-cost benefits that* (name of client) *enrolled in at my department. You have the ability to receive a free quote. What is your date of birth....*

*Note: At this point, an agent should start at the beginning of your Sales Presentation Script just like you normally would with any lead contact.)

Policy Conservation

I do not place any follow up call to the client a few days after making the sale on purpose. Why?

First of all, the insurance company is going to mail the policy directly to the client within 10 business days. A final expense phone sales agent does not have to personally deliver the policy, since our customers are usually several states away. If the client does not see their policy in 10-14 business days (which never happens), the client will let their agent know.

Secondly, a follow up phone call from an agent a few days following a sale only begs the client who is experiencing buyer's remorse to cancel their policy with the agent while on the phone with them.

The last thing a successful agent wants to do is to facilitate the cancellation of a sold policy, unless the client initiates it and makes a direct cancellation request. Let the client be one to call the agent who sold them a policy, if they desire to cancel.

Once a client receives their policy in the mail within 10 business days, and reviews their actual policy, they most always keep it.

Approximately 5-10% of all policies sold by a final expense agent will need some "special attention" later. Things happen.

To conserve your book of business, an agent must schedule some time to handle policy "hic cups". This could include: policy cancellations, policy declines, bank draft issues (insufficient funds, client changing banks, wrong premiums drafted, changing draft dates), client requests to change or add beneficiaries, follow up health questions, securing medical records of the client, etc.

It is my professional estimation that it is worth an agent's time to pay close attention to and resolve these issues between the insured and the insurance company. In my mind, a policy conserved is a policy sold.

However, it is also my professional opinion that these policy conservation matters should *not* be handled during prime selling hours of the day Monday through Thursday. It should all be handled on Friday, or at the close of each business day around 4pm EST (after an agent has made one or more sales).

Nothing can put an agent in a foul mood quicker than negatory policy issues. This is why an expert final expense agent will never handle these challenges at the beginning of a selling day.

It is supremely important for an expert agent to begin each selling day with an upbeat, positive disposition. This is why all policy conservation issues should be handled later in the day after an agent has made one or more daily sales.

Older ("B") Lead Script - Initial Introduction

Dr. Clark's "Older Leads" Sales Script:
www.finalexpensesuccess.com/sales-products

    Calling through "B" leads (Free leads over 30 days old) is like trying to find low-hanging fruit that is ready to be harvested. All "B" leads are not ripe for a sale, so the agent is locating just the right customer who will allow an agent to harvest a sale.

    Almost 20-30% of "B" leads have never been contacted, due to reasons discussed in Chapter One. Another 30% of "B" leads are **buyers** who simply did not buy from the original agent who contacted them.

    Sometimes a "B" lead sale simply takes a second look, another agent, or a different personality, for the customer to feel comfortable in making a buying decision. Sometimes an agent could not qualify a customer with one particular insurance carrier, but another agent may be able to qualify the customer with a different insurance carrier.

    If the purchase was not made up front with the original salesperson, remember that a sale is statistically closed after the 5th contact.

    This means when I call a "B" lead, I may be just the right agent the customer was looking for to purchase coverage. What an agent should be looking for while contacting "B" leads is someone who will give the agent the "time of day".

    If an agent locates someone who will give him time to deliver a free quote, the agent can make a sales presentation. When an agent makes a sales presentation, there is always a 50/50 chance to close a sale.

5-8 sales presentations per day is what generates one or more sales per day.

    Although an agent will follow the same Sales Presentation Script for "B" leads that is normally utilized for "A" leads, the initial up front introduction is key to opening up a conversation. Because a "B" lead customer may have been contacted by a previous agent, it is important for the next agent to make a different appeal to the customer than the original agent. That is, approach the customer in a "follow up" manner, not as an original call.

For example, an expert agent never says, "I received your card in the mail requesting information...", because that is how the previous agent introduced himself to the customer.

Here are various, effective talking points of introduction for a "B" lead:

Agent: *Hi* (first name of customer). *This is* (name of agent) *from the Final Expense Department...*

- *We are following up on your request for benefits here at my department.*
- *It is my job to follow up with your case.*
- *Our records here indicate that you have not received the benefits that you requested.*
- *Did someone contact you already about the benefits you requested? Why were they not able to help you receive your benefits?*
- *We'd like to know - Did you want the benefits for yourself, or may we have your permission to share the benefits with someone else?*

Always listen for the customer's challenge, objection, or reason why they did not move forward with the original agent. Usually a customer will let an agent know what happened right up front. This is key! Now, the current agent can handle the customer's buying obstacle right up front!

If the customer's obstacle can be overcome with the agent's professional assistance, here are effective talking points for the agent to utilize:

- *This is not a problem. I am sorry that you were not able to move forward with the benefits that you are entitled to here. I can take care of it for you right now.*
- *Let's see exactly what you qualify for.*

- *I apologize for the previous representative who was not able to help you. It is my job to follow up with you and make sure that you get the benefits you are entitled to here.*
- *It is a good thing you are talking to me now. I will be able to secure available benefits that you requested there in* (city of customer).

Customer Objections / Agent Rebuttals

Dr. Clark's complete Agent Rebuttal / Customer Objection Script: **www.finalexpensesuccess.com/objection-rebuttal-sales-script**

Objection: *I want to wait/need more time to make a decision.*
Rebuttal: *Suppose I have a big Crystal Ball in front of us here. We could look into the Crystal Ball and be able to predict the day of our death. We would then get life insurance one month before death, so that we are paying the least amount of cost and getting the most amount of benefit. Since there is no such Crystal Ball, this is why we purchase life insurance. No one knows when death will occur. You can wait as long as you want to, but people who wait, wait too late. One trip to the doctor, or one trip down a flight of stairs, can eliminate your chances forever to qualify for life insurance. Does it sound smart to you to wait without knowing when death will occur and without being able to predict the future?*

Objection: *I want to wait/need more time to make a decision.*
Rebuttal: *How much time do you need to think about it?*
Objection: *Well, I just need some time to go over everything and figure out which one is best for me.*
Rebuttal: *Sure. Go ahead and decide for yourself for a few moments. I'll be working at my desk here. Just let me know when you decide which plan works best for you.*
Objection: *Can I just call you back tomorrow? I just need more time to think about it.*
Rebuttal: (name of customer), *how old are you? 68? Ok. You have already picked out the $5,000 plan at $35 per month. You have told me that the $35 premium would fit*

comfortably into your budget. (name of customer), *you are into your 69th year of life. You have been thinking about death since mid life, for at least two decades now. How much more time do need to think about it? You have (little or no) coverage right now. Your son, John, would be your beneficiary. How much would John pay out of his own pocket for your funeral costing $10,000, if something should happen to you tonight? How much would John be required to pay out?*
Client: *About $5,000.*
Rebuttal: *Ok. Now, how much would John have to pay for your $10,000 funeral, if you made one premium payment on this $5,000 plan, and if something should happen to you tonight? How much would John be required to pay?*
Client: *Nothing.*
Rebuttal: *Exactly. Does it sound smart to you to wait, or to put your coverage into effect right now?*

Objection: *I want to wait/need more time to make a decision.*
Rebuttal: *The truth is,* (name of customer), *you can wait another* (**age** of customer) *years. Makes no difference to me. You have to go through me in order to apply for the state approved benefits.*
I have some guidelines that I go by here. I am not allowed to "hold the benefits" open for anyone. The lowest premium rates can change unpredictably on people who wait. If you are serious about permanently protecting your family's future, I don't need any money today, but I do need to qualify you for the one that you want. I can lock these benefits into place permanently that you now qualify for, so that your plan never changes after today.
I speak to two types of people. Those who say later, "I wish I had", and those who say "I'm glad I did". Which person sounds smart to you?

Objection: *I want to wait/need more time to make a decision.*
Rebuttal: *This not important tomorrow. This is important today. The more you get into the habit of putting off, the*

LESS opportunity you'll get to be able to take care of your future. We can't do this all the time. Right now, you are positioned to lose large cash benefits that you qualify for at lowest premium rates, unless you allow yourself to move forward today. Will you choose poorly or wisely? How can I help you win, and not lose this permanent protection for your family?

Objection: *I want to wait/need more time to make a decision.*

Rebuttal: *Do you want your family's LAST MEMORY of you on this earth, to be that you gave them thousands of dollars of debt? Are you going to waste this opportunity and more time to make sure your responsibility is covered? Or, will you allow me to move forward with you to create a lasting memory on this earth that you can feel proud of?*

Objection: *I want to wait/need more time to make a decision.*

Rebuttal: *As a Licensed Field Underwriter, I spend quality time helping folks who want immediate cash benefits. I certainly do not want to come across as being rude, but I do have many people clamoring for my attention each day, more than I can get to sometimes. You have several people "standing in line" behind you. I am not allowed to hold the benefits or the lowest premiums open for anyone. This lets me know who I need to spend my time with. IF YOU ARE SERIOUS about this valuable life-long protection for you and your family, I will accept your application, if you are willing to do whatever it takes to work it out in a way that is comfortable today. So, if you want my professional help, I am on the phone with you now. I will spend as much time as you need to make your decision, while you've got me on the phone with you. Do you want me to move forward with you to provide a permanent solution for burial costs? I don't want you to get lost in the shuffle here. Go ahead and pick a plan that is right for you, and we will set it at the price and on the day of the month that is comfortable for you.*

> *Some people fold after making one timid request. They quit too soon. In sales there are usually four or five "no's" before you get a "yes".*
>
> **Jack Canfield** [1]

More Effective Closing Rebuttals

Objection: *I just don't know if this is right for me.*
Rebuttal: (name of customer), *you have $7,000 coverage in front of you that becomes the very first money your family sees within 48 hours to 5 days at the time of your passing. Most large term policies over $50,000 take 6 weeks to 6 months before the family sees the first penny. Yours will pay out immediately during the worst week of your family's life, when they lose you.*
100% of the benefits are paid directly to John, your son, immediately. 100% cash. It will not be touched by the Federal Government or be taxable. It will not go through state probate.
Even though you have a heart condition, high blood pressure, and diabetes, we are not penalizing you with a 2-3 year waiting period for coverage like other insurance companies would treat you to. You have 100% full coverage from day one, just like anyone in their 20's with perfect health. There is no waiting period.
You also qualify for our discounted rates for being a nonsmoker. You also have the extra Grandchild Benefit. All grandchildren are covered under your plan. You also have Cash Value inside of your plan at no charge. This will grow every month almost like a savings account and will pay your premiums for you in case of a financial emergency, so you never lose your protection.
Your coverage will automatically DOUBLE in case of an accidental death, without having to apply for it. $5,000 becomes $10,000 that will pay to John immediately in full upon an accidental death.
What is that worth to you, (name of customer)? Is that worth a $40 per month premium payment to you?

Objection: *We live in such a bad economy. Should I take this coverage now?*
Rebuttal: *I appreciate your honesty,* (name of customer). *The economy hasn't been bad just today. Think of how hard it would be on your family if they suffered your loss, and then had to come up with an additional $5-7-10,000? The funeral home does not do business for free. Think how hard it would be if your premium payments kept going up, because you waited. Your plan here will never change at the coverage amount and premium you sign up for. Then, your family will always be protected at monthly premiums you can afford.*

Objection: *Are you sure this is for real?*
(*** THIS REBUTTAL SHOULD **ONLY** BE USED AS A VERY LAST RESORT OPTION WHEN ALL ELSE HAS FAILED)
Rebuttal: *I assure you this is very much for real. Have you heard of our 30 Day Free Look Period? We send out your policy right away. Within 10 business days you will have your actual policy in your hands. You then have 30 days to look over your policy and the opportunity to cancel it, if you are not completely satisfied. We are simply applying for the coverage now. It is not permanent unless you decide to keep it.*

Chapter Four

Sales Presentation
Agent Weekly Schedule
Diet
Faith

*Sell from the heart,
not the head.*

*The more a customer buys INTO you;
the more a customer will buy FROM you.*

Troy Clark

Sales Presentation of Final Expense

I want to clearly lay out in this section my proven, field-tested Sales Presentation Script MANUAL that invokes customer interest, clarity of benefits, and rebuts customer objections or concerns.

Important is the order of conversation. That is, certain things should be discussed at certain times between a customer and an agent – and not a moment too soon, or too late. A successful sale is almost like a solar eclipse. Certain things have to line up in a certain way at certain times for one sale to take place.

This section addresses these crucial factors.

There are two things an agent needs to sell final expense insurance successfully: 1) a very good Sales Presentation, 2) a work ethic. Either one by itself is incomplete.

Work ethic is addressed in Chapter 5 under the heading, *"Straight Talk and Selling Final Expense"*. So, let us now grasp the meaning of a very good Sales Presentation.

Dr. Clark's superior Sales Presentation Script MANUAL at ***www.finalexpensesuccess.com/sales-script-manual*** is so effective that a total stranger (a customer) will lend to another total stranger (an agent) their bank account information to put a policy in force, sight unseen. It is simply amazing. The Sales Presentation Script alone is not enough, however. It is all in how an agent utilizes it.

Because key verbiage within our Sales Script was inserted by design from my very own sales technique, along with other National Top Producers winning sales verbiage, I understand the purpose of each and every page. Each page accomplishes its own unique and crucial agreement "tie downs" between an agent and a customer.

A customer never sees the end. They only hear the benefit information from the agent, and begin to understand the value of the benefits as it applies to them, one bit of good news at a time.

Our Sales Script is like a refreshing, trickling stream flowing into every crack and crevice of a customer's apprehension over personal debt left behind at their death. The wave of benefit information received from a final expense sales agent surges the customer ahead into a reservoir of assurance at the projected end of life's journey.

Our Sales Script is the ebb-n-flow of a perceived income stream that carries the customer across financial hardship onto the shore of individual fulfillment of their final, financial responsibilities.

Picture if you will, a large brook or stream running through the middle of the woods. It is much too wide to leap across. Together, both the customer and the agent stand at the edge of the stream. There is only way across. Large rocks, or stepping stones, are scattered within the stream.

Each page of the Sales Script is a stepping stone. Some stones are wide and flat. Some are slanted and moss-covered. Some are small enough for only one foot to step on. Some can stand 2 or 3 people all at once. All are slippery. One wrong move could end the fun of crossing the stream safely together.

The lead card is the initial "treasure map" that peaks the interest of the customer to acquire into benefits that rest on the other side of the stream. The customer's desire is to find out what is on the other side waiting for them. So, it becomes the agent's job to lead and take care of the customer, as they cross the stream together.

An expert agent initiates the first step onto the nearest stepping stone, which is the first page of the Sales Script. The agent then assists the customer to join him. The big idea here is to *make sure the customer is with the agent*, before stepping to the next rock or proceeding to the next page of the script.

Many agents plow through pages of the Sales Script only to turn around at the close and find the customer nowhere in sight, meaning: not ready to make a buying decision, because the customer is still standing on the opposite side of the stream. You forgot to make sure the

customer crosses the stream with you! Each page of the script, each stepping stone, accomplishes something needful for both the customer and the agent. Both agent and customer must be on the same page of the script and take each step together!
Never move forward, until you both are moving forward **together.**
The agent steps forward. The customer follows.
Each page of the Sales Script is one, small step forward. Yet, the customer may want to stop and talk about other "distractions in the woods", or matters of personal safely, while crossing the stream with the agent.

An expert agent will not panic when this happens (Notice I said <u>when</u>, not "if" it happens).

You already know the customer cannot advance to the next stepping stone (or page) in the Sales Script, without YOU moving forward first. So, stop, when the customer stops. Use whatever concern or point of interest the customer brings to your attention as an OPPORTUNITY to alleviate the customer's concern, and win your customer's trust in you as a leader.

This is done by explaining the benefits more clearly, answering questions, or handling a customer's objections. Reassure the customer that your thoughts are for the best interest of their family.

The *big purchase* decision at the close is made up of several **little decisions**, called "tie downs", throughout the Sales Script. Each page of my Sales Presentation Script MANUAL is engineered (by design) to accomplish these important "tie downs", or agreements, between the customer and agent.

A skillful agent will allow a customer to secure information about end-of-life benefits that they requested, while "tying down" the sale at the same time within a sequence of small agreements.

Why are small, "tie down" agreements between the customer and agent important throughout the course of an agent's Sales Presentation? Each small, "tie down" agreement on each page of our Sales Script specifically "nips in the bud" all major customer objections one-at-a-time!

Either an agent can handle many different objections at the close when it comes time for the agent to bring a customer to the point of a buying decision, or objections can be virtually **ELLIMINATED BEFOREHAND !!!**

Each "tie down" agreement on each page of our Sales Script addresses and overcomes a specific type of potential customer objection. This makes many different types of potential objections nonexistent at the close when it is time for the customer to make a buying decision, because the objection has been previously and effectively squelched by a skillful agent!

The reasons why National Top Producers have a high closing ratio (70%-80% = 7-8 policies sold out of 10 presentations), is because an expert agent hears only 1 or 2 or NO objections at all at the close of a sale. The potential customer objections were masterfully handled throughout the Sales Presentation by the agent, *before the customer ever had a chance to bring them up.*

There are only one or two types of objections that an expert final expense telesales agent will face at the close, if the "tie down" agreements with the customer have previously been accomplished on the part of a professional agent.

Which would you prefer to handle at the close, 10 types of objections, or 1-2 types of objections? 1-2 is a much smaller number to deal with. The difference is to eliminate potential customer objections in the Sales Script *without the customer knowing it* in the form of small, seeming insignificant "tie down" agreements between the customer and agent.

"Tie down" questions on each page of our Sales Script are identified for an agent to focus on. NEVER bypass these critical questions. It is CRUCIAL for the customer to "sell themselves" on your product by finding common ground with the agent that both agree upon. This is what "tie downs" ultimately accomplish.

Presentation/Schedule/Diet/Faith 153

THE MORE A CUSTOMER AGREES WITH AN AGENT THROUGHOUT THE SALES PRESENTATION, THE MORE LIKELY A CUSTOMER WILL AGREE TO PURCHASE COVERAGE AT THE CLOSE OF THE SALE.

These scripted questions are the key that unlock every door for both the customer and the agent to be able to move forward together. Always together! As we stroll through each section of an effective sales presentation together, I will point out the specific customer objection that is being "nipped in the bud" by the customer/agent "tie down" agreement.

It is the wise telesales agent who masters the small "tie downs" on each page of the script, rather than only focusing on the big purchase decision at the close.

Beginning with the Opening Page, the lead card is verified by the agent with the corresponding customer. The 2 potential customer objections at the close of a sale, which will be "nipped in the bud" in the Opening Page are as follows:

I never sent a card in the mail.
I was checking on benefits for my _____, not for me.

Whether or not the customer remembers filling out then mailing in the lead card is inconsequential to the more important "tie down" at this time.

Maybe the card was mailed by someone else other than who the agent is speaking to. Maybe the customer really *does* remember mailing the card, but does not initially want to own up to it, because they think the agent is a telemarketer. Maybe the customer needs a moment to dust the cobwebs out of their memory bank.

The important thing for the agent is to identify that a card was mailed by someone who knew how to sign the customer's name, who wrote down the customer's date of birth, and who lives at the address on the card. A lot of times I may ask the customer, *"I wonder who would know how to sign your name, know your phone number, and know how to write down your date of birth? I wonder who that could be"? (H-m-m-m…)*

Regardless, the "tie down" question asked by the agent inquires, *"Now, were you checking into benefits for yourself, or for someone else?"*

This innocent question asked by an agent to identify the buyer is perceived by the customer as a simple verification for speaking to the correct person. However, when the customer answers (as they do 98% of the time) that they were checking into benefits for themselves, this actually becomes the customer's initial OWNERSHIP of the benefits.

This is a "tie down"! To ultimately purchase a plan for coverage, the customer must be given the opportunity to **take initial ownership** of their benefits. There will be no sale in the end without an up-front, conscious connection on the part of the customer to the benefits they desire. Here is where this connection is first made.

An expert final expense agent knows **not** to move forward to the next page in the Sales Presentation Script, until the customer and the benefits have joined together here.

If the person the agent is speaking to is not the person who inquired into the benefits, the agent must locate that person. Simply ask for the correct person to be handed the telephone.

Always begin from the top of the Opening Page of the Sales Script with the correct person on the telephone. Verify the information on the lead card the customer filled out. Then "tie down" the customer's inquiry into benefits that they requested on themselves.

After doing so, the next page of the Sales Script will allow the agent to officially introduce himself to the customer and explain why the agent is calling to share benefits the customer requested.

The 3 potential customer objections at the close of a sale, which will be "nipped in the bud" on the Who I Am Page are as follows:

Presentation/Schedule/Diet/Faith

- I do not speak to telemarketers.
- I need information in writing sent to me before I can make a decision.
- I do not have the money today. Or,
- I thought the benefits were free.

The "tie down" agreements on this page in the Sales Script will alleviate any unrest in the customer's disposition about telemarketers. It will also curb a customer's indifference to ask for the benefit information to be sent to them in the mail, because the customer is not comfortable with the agent yet. Most importantly, the customer will realize that there is a monthly premium involved, although the customer has no need to spend any money today to apply for the benefits that they request for their family.

A wise telesales expert also realizes that it is vital to "hook the customer" up front with curious interest before the customer has a chance to get bored or express non-interest due to, again, avoiding what the customer perceives as being a telemarketer.

The exact verbiage of how an agent accomplishes this is in found in Chapter 3 under the heading - *Who I Am and What I Do.*

So as to lend respect to the customer's time, the customer is asked by the agent, *"May I share with you IN ONE MINUTE who I am, what these benefits are exactly, and how you (the customer) may apply for them here at my department?"*

This gives the customer a chance to **AGREE** to a realistic and doable timeframe in conversation. What the customer does not realize is how good the benefits are going to sound, how fortunate they are to be speaking with a caring licensed final expense expert, as well as a painless process to sign up for the benefits now, while an agent is on the telephone with them.

These great-sounding benefits the customer inquired into should sound impossible to say "no" to within the first couple of minutes of an expert agent explaining it to them.

The secret to selling is to *sell the secret*.
Your benefits should sound like an untold "mystery" to the customer. Intriguing. Captivating. Your final expense plan should initially come across as the "best kept secret" in the entire funeral protection industry.
Interject words picture and questions that invoke curiosity:

> ➤ Are you aware that we have no-cost, extra benefits in your area that come directly by qualifying for one of our plans?
> ➤ Did you know that as a Licensed Field Underwriter, I can qualify folks who have been rejected and refused by everyone else they have tried to get coverage with?
> ➤ Remind me to share with you later how your entire funeral is paid for, after only one premium payment!
> ➤ Did you know that we have the technology at my Department, so that NO PAPERWORK is required for you to fill out, if you qualify for one of our plans here?
> ➤ Don't let me forget to share with you how your family and friends can also receive the same benefits, without them having to send a card in to my department.

These thought-provoking questions create intrigue in the customer's mind, as never-before-heard-of benefits that the agent may explain in greater detail later, if the customer qualifies.

Make qualifying for one of your plans a "mystery of anticipation". This keeps the customer on the "edge of their seat" and eager to move forward with you!

If an agent does not accomplish this within the first moments of conversation, every excuse in the book will be dished out to the agent by the customer to avoid further conversation:

- *I am too busy now. I'm not interested.*
- *Can you just send it in the mail?*
- *I did not send in a card.*
- *I probably do not qualify.*
- *How much does it cost?*

These customer "balkings" can all be "nipped in the bud" by a skillful agent, depending on how well an agent addresses specific points of benefit information up front. These are crucial points to be addressed by the agent:

✓ Agent Title and Department calling from.
✓ State-approved CASH benefits for funeral and burial protection.
✓ Benefit payout immediately within 5 days after death, if you qualify.
✓ There are some health questions and a FREE Quote to qualify for your requested benefits.
✓ Benefits are secured for your family by applying for them right over the telephone **without spending any money today**.
✓ After the customer applies for their benefits, they will receive a "Welcome Packet" within 2-3 business days, and their actual policy within 10 business days.

Now comes the all-important "tie down" question: *"Is this what you are needing my help with today?"* If the customer answers, "Yes", the agent knows that they have a buyer on the phone within the first 5-10 minutes of the conversation!

A good follow up "tie down" question is: *"Is there anywhere you need to be this morning/afternoon? Do you have any appointments today?"* If the customer answers, "No", an agent may proceed forward with the question, *"Can you share a few minutes with me, while you've got me on the phone, to see exactly what you can qualify for?"*

A "Yes" answer to these simple "tie down" questions does several things.

At this point both the agent and customer have made an initial understand and agreement about **1)**who the agent is, **2)**where he is calling from, **3)**what the (final expense) benefits are exactly, **4)**how the customer will receive the benefit information they requested, **5)**how to apply for the benefits desired without spending any money today, and **6)**all information sent in writing to the customer to validate what has been discussed.

If a customer answers, "No", to the "tie down" question, *"Is this what you are needing my help with today?"*, the agent respectfully bids the customer a good day and politely hang ups the telephone to then call on the next lead prospect.

If a customer answers, "Maybe", or "I don't know", to the same "tie down" question, perhaps the agent needs to further investigate the customer's reason for mailing the response card. After doing so, an agent must never move forward to the next page of the Sales Script, until the customer acknowledges that they specifically desire the agent's assistance with benefits for end-of-life funeral and burial protection.

If an agent addresses a customer's predictable points of concern early on in the Sales Script, I guarantee almost 100% of the time that the customer will NOT use certain objections at the close, when it comes time to make a buying decision.

This is imminently important to making ONE sale!!

Sometimes a customer may resort to certain buying objections at the close of an agent's presentation, *not because the objections are real or actually apply to the customer*, but because there is hinge of DOUBT in the mind of the customer about *other* things, such as: who the agent really is, where they are really calling from, what information the customer will get in writing, and if the customer has to spend any money today to apply for benefits today.

A customer objection many times is just a customer's way of letting an agent know that an agent forgot to alleviate basic upfront customer concerns.

There are basic and legitimate concerns in the mind of EVERY CUSTOMER from the first "hello" moment in a conversation over the telephone. If these customer concerns are not addressed by the agent upfront, they will most likely show up later in the form of an objection to the agent at the close, and jeopardize the entire sale. An expert final expense sales agent knows this, and takes care of basic customer concerns that lurk initially "under the radar" in the mind of a customer, before they have a chance to surface at the close and torpedo the customer's buying decision.

This is what the "Who I Am and What I Do" page accomplishes within our superior Sales Presentation Script.

Following the "Who I Am and What I Do" portion of our Sales Script is the initial "Warm-Up and Need Establishment" of the customer.

At this point in the Sales Script, the following potential customer objections at the close are "nipped in the bud": (In a customer's mind, not vocalized)

- This person does not care about me or my family.
- He/She only wants my money (a sale).
- I already have enough coverage.
- I have no need for the coverage you are offering to me.

It is the objective of an expert agent to further inquire about the customer's situation and need for burial protection and what the customer desires to accomplish with the benefits they hope to qualify for.

Exact verbiage is found in Chapter 3 under the headings "Customer Warm Up" and "Identify Customer Need". My complete Sales Script MANUAL is shared with agents at:
www.finalexpensesuccess.com/sales-script-manual

The essential "tie down" during the "Warm Up" period of the conversation between an agent and a customer is a more personal exchange of information about one another. An agent may initiate this by letting the customer know that as a professional you desire to build meaningful, life-long relationships with each of your clients. It is extremely important that a customer feel their family is being **cared for** and **cared about** by a licensed insurance professional.

Agent: *I want to give you access to my private phone line and get to know your situation a little better, before I share the benefits with you and your family. How does that sound?*
Customer: *Sounds great.*
Agent: *How long have you been living in (city)…?*

After spending 5-10 minutes chatting over the "Warm Up" items listed in Chapter 3, an expert agent will then pivot the conversation to the inevitable "customer need" factor.

Agent: *Now, folks, there is something I always ask at this point. Tell me,* **what do you feel your needs are? What were your thoughts and concerns about your family when you sent the card in to my Department?**
Client: *Well, we just did not want our children (or family) to have a financial hardship fall back on them, if something should happen to us. We want our funeral to be paid for.*
Agent: *Do I hear you saying that you just want a plan that is small, affordable, pays out immediately no matter what, just to cover a basic, decent funeral?*
Client: *Yes, that's all we want.*
Agent: *Ok. I want to be sure that I am on the same page that you are on, going in the same direction that you are going. That is why I was asking.*
Client: *Ok.*
Agent: *We all know that it is expensive to live. It is also expensive to die. It is not something that "might" happen. It is something that is* **going to happen**. *It is always*

easier to pay a little bit at a time, than it is to pay $10,000 all at once, right?
Client: *That's right.*
Agent: *Well, folks, I do feel comfortable moving forward with you, because it sounds like that you care about your family. You want to get something in place that is permanent, small, affordable, and pays out immediately - no matter what - because you don't want your loved ones to have to dig into their own pockets on top of all the emotional stress of losing you. Does that sound like you?*
Client: *Yes. That's right.*

The question "Does that sound like you?" is the "tie down" agreement opportunity. A "Yes" answer by the customer is, in effect, a customer saying that they agree with the agent and wish to proceed to the next level of qualifying for benefits. It is a conscious permission by the customer given to the agent to fill their need for burial expense protection.

Without a customer disclosing **why** they are seeking coverage, the agent has no chance of making the sale. To overcome the apprehension, fear, or anxiety of the customer over funeral expenses, it becomes a necessary skill of the agent to correctly identify and validate the customer's need.

When a customer verbalizes for a few moments why they sent in the card requesting benefit information, as well as what they feel their needs are for burial protection, the customer is actually **selling themselves** on the agent's product.

Establishing a customer's realistic need becomes the anchor to the sale.

Upon establishing a definite customer need, the pre-qualifying Health Questions create an aura of anticipation to see exactly what benefits the customer can qualify for.

Two potential customer objections at the close "nipped in the bud" during the Medical Questions Page of the Sales Script are as follows:

My health probably disqualifies me.
I do not have a bank account.

To set an official and respectable tone for the Health Questions, a customer should be made aware, before questions are asked by an agent, that although there is no physical examination required, this is a state-regulated program in (customer's state of residence), so there is a standard MIB (Medical Information Bureau) check on all answers that the customer provides about their health. The explanation to the customer about the MIB is detailed in Chapter 3 under the heading, "Health Questions".

It is critical to ask the customer not only the 8-10 prequalifying Health Questions, but also an exact list of prescription medications the customer is currently taking. This ensures utmost accuracy on the Free Quote given later by the agent. How?

A final expense sales agent is normally provided a "Med Chart" List. The Med Chart displays every major U.S. Prescription by name and lists the physical conditions related to each prescription. This Med Chart allows an agent to narrow down exactly what physical condition the customer is taking for each prescription they list, so that an agent can make an instant and accurate assessment of which final expense plan the customer qualifies for on the spot, without having to put the customer on hold for a day or two to find out otherwise.

The Med Chart is a powerfully effective tool for an agent to be able to make an accurate, instant sale TODAY.

It is also essential to note that while the customer is in a "question-answer" frame of mind that a "tie down" question is asked at the close of Medical Health Questions. Customer bank account information is initially verified by the agent here for this reason.

Agent: *Thank you, Mary, for your honesty. This does conclude our Medical Questions.*
Client: *You're Welcome.*

Agent: *Now, your ability to secure coverage depends on your health and one other thing. Mary, Unlike most policies who do a credit check, we simply go by the "honor system" here at the Department. Have you bounced any checks in the past month? Do you have an account in good standing?*
Client: *Oh, Yes.*
Agent: *Super!*

A valid customer bank account is briefly verified at this point by an agent. Exact verbiage to artfully handle this delicate part of the sale, is within Dr. Clark's Sales Presentation Script MANUAL: ***www.finalexpensesuccess.com/sales-script-manual***

Policy benefits are next, shared in specific detail by an agent with the customer. It is at this point that perhaps the most important "tie down" is locked into place – the "Decision Maker" tie down.

The primary customer objection at the close that is "nipped in the bud" on the Benefits Page of our Sales Script is as follows:

> I need to talk this over with --- (son, daughter, spouse, etc.), before I make my decision.

As articulated with exact verbiage in Chapter 3 under the heading "Benefits", an agent is curbing a major objection at the close by making sure all decision makers are on the telephone now.

When the customer verifies that they are able to make their own financial decisions, and no one else is needed to help the customer make a decision, it is a green light for the agent to move forward to share the benefit information and Free Quote the customer has been patiently waiting for.

I cannot stress how all-important it is to be sure that **the customer convinces the agent** at this point of their own ability to make sound financial decisions all by themselves . The reason is not because the agent doesn't believe the customer can decide for themselves. More importantly, it invests the customer into making a decision sooner rather than later, because there is no one else they need to consult. This increases the odds of making an instant sale in favor of the agent. It also lends confidence that a decision can be reached today in favor of a needy customer.

The "Decision Maker" tie down question is asked first on the Benefits Page of the Sales Script (exact verbiage Chapter 3 under *Benefits*). After the agent and customer both agree together that the customer is fit to make their own financial decisions, the benefits may be explained in detail by a wise agent.

During the beginning "Warm Up" Page of the Sales Script, if you recall in Chapter 3, an expert agent will wisely create an immediate curiosity in the mind of the customer by asking the customer to remind the agent later about **no-cost, extra benefits** that connect to the customer's family life or situation, if they qualify (Grandchild Benefit, Cash Draft Benefit, Cash Value Benefit, etc.).

Now that the customer does qualify for a specific final expense coverage plan, an expert agent will recall the no-cost benefits alluded to earlier during the "Warm Up" Page of the Sales Script and relate them to the customer. This adds value not only to the product, but also to the agent's professionalism, in the grateful mind of a customer.

The "Pre-Close" Page certainly continues another important "tie down", but more as a positive reinforcement to the customer, rather than in the form of a question.

An agent is also busy using a Rate Calculator, provided to our telesales agents, to instantly figure the 3 Option Quote to be given to the waiting customer. Multitasking is a useful skill on the part of an agent. An expert agent is complimenting the customer on qualifying for the coverage, as well as the additional benefits, while at the same time calculating the free quote coverage amounts and monthly premiums.

Complimentary verbiage to the customer within an agent's Sales Presentation buys a few moments of extra

Presentation/Schedule/Diet/Faith

time for the agent to calculate the customer's coverage amounts and premium rates.

If the compliments shared from the agent to the customer are done just right, the customer will acknowledge them with a heartfelt, *"Thank you"*! This is a "tie down" nonetheless in the form of mutual agreement.

IT IS NOW TIME TO CLOSE THE SALE!

Pause for a moment, if you will, and re-think the series of previous "tie downs" between the agent and the customer to arrive at this closing point in the Sales Presentation Script.

The customer first verified the card with the agent and agreed to the agent's inquiry that they were checking into benefits for themselves on the "Opening" Page.

Next, the customer listened to the agent share briefly "Who I Am and What I Do", agreeing with the agent thereafter that this is the professional assistance the customer is requesting.

The "Warm Up" and "Customer Need" Page of the Sales Script opened up the agent to the customer's family situation, background, and a *real need* for burial protection, as well as what the customer desires to accomplish with the benefits they hope to qualify for.

The pre-qualifying "Health Questions" are a sobering necessity to "tie down" the customer's exact plan for coverage. An initial bank account validation is also acknowledged between the agent and the customer.

Just before the "Benefits" Page is thoroughly reviewed by the agent, the financial decision maker is established to be the customer and no one else.

In the "Pre-Close" Page of the Sales Script the 3 Option free quote is laid out plainly for the customer to write down. As an agent asks the customer if they desire to look any higher coverage or not, the customer will "tie down" themselves to the benefits with a request for a higher quote or to simply stay put with the free quote as it is.

Finally, the complimentary acknowledgment by the agent to the customer's qualification for coverage, as well as no-cost benefits, leads into the close of the sale here at the "Close" Page of the Sales Script.

Now, to make the sale, an agent must be willing to "ask for the sale".

*If you are not moving closer to what you want
in sales (or in life),
you probably aren't doing enough asking.*
Jack Canfield 1

What does it means to "ask for the sale"? It means that the agent must lasso the customer with a final "tie down" agreement to purchase the plan.

At this time, the big buying decision does not seem so ominously huge to the customer, if the agent has properly made several previous buying-signal, tie-down agreements together with the customer.

At this time, a buying decision seems to the customer to be simply another agreement between the agent and the customer in the sequence of several previous "green light" agreements.

At this time, the agent has leverage to ask for the sale:

- Which one of these 3 plans appeal to you the most?
- Which plan would take care of your family, if something should happen to you tonight?
- Which plan do you want my Department to put into place permanently for your family?
- Which plan do you want to comfort your family with as your last act of love?
- Which one of these 3 plans fit best into your lifestyle and budget?

If a customer is ready to decide, they will immediately point out the specific plan that is right for them. On the other hand, some customers need more reassuring. Objections, concerns, and questions from the customer are an excellent opportunity for an expert agent to add value to the customer's situation and alleviate their fears (the source of all objections). ALWAYS end every agent rebuttal to every customer objection, concern, or question with **asking for the sale!**

Over and over again an agent should keep asking for the sale no matter how many concerns the customer has. The agent must keep asking, until the customer picks a plan for themselves.

Never take for granted the sale is won before the customer picks a plan for themselves. Again, the series of previous "tie down" decisions between the customer and the agent make it much easier for both to reach a buying agreement at the close of the sale.

Agent Weekly Schedule

People do not plan to fail, but most people fail to plan.

Dr. Clark's Agent Sales Schedule:
www.finalexpensesuccess.com/sales-products

It was so frustrating. Why was I not enjoying my insurance business? Within the first few months as a final expense phone sales agent, I was selling several policies per week, generating $1,000-$3,500 weekly income.

Yet, I hated Monday morning. I loathed the work of making several presentations to several customers before making one sale. Even though I was skillful at it, churning out one or more policies per day, my reluctance to start each new day serving final expense plans reached a daunting low.

What was happening to me? I sat in the chair behind my desk with my face down in both hands literally weeping morning after morning. I knew the reality of dealing with customers was running crosswise to the grain of my soul.

Enter my wise father. I had a talk with dear ole' dad about this. He is a busy and successful minister, and a wise counselor. We pin-pointed together what was happening. We discovered that I was handling too many of life's obligations within my own mind. At the time, I did not adhere to or work from a weekly schedule.

During each day, I was mentally jumbling altogether business expectations, personal issues, relationships, all of life's little "stressors" - all at the same time. My business life was overlapping with my personal life and vice versa.

While I was serving and selling final expense policies, I had a million other things begging to be done that weighed heavy on my brain, constantly gnawing at the back of my brain.

Because my central nervous system was overloaded at the beginning of each new day (by trying to mentally figure out all that I need to accomplish to be successful), the tears leaked out my inner stress of not knowing how it was all going to get done. The solution came in my father's simple advice.

"Have you ever written out a weekly schedule," he inquired. *"Why do I need a written-out, daily schedule?"*, I mused. Its purpose, I was told, was to take all of life's demands off of my mind, while I am working, selling, and serving final expense policies.

THIS BECAME THE **SECRET REASON** TO MY FUTURE
SUCCESS !!!

The reality is, I am *no better of a salesperson than **you are***. All of my success as a final expense sales professional does not come from natural ability, not brains, not talent, definitely not luck, and not from some mystical inbred advantage, but rather my success is a pre-planned result from a weekly agent schedule. Living by a weekly schedule became my chance to enjoy what I do, and succeed at it.

My daily/weekly schedule took everything off of my mind, so that I could focus on one thing at a time, **and one thing only**, while selling final expense insurance.

Presentation/Schedule/Diet/Faith

This replaced life's stressors with structure. All of life's obligations were strategically placed within my weekly schedule to be taken care of in due course of each day, each week. This liberated my mind.

Right now, without a weekly selling schedule, a typical self employed insurance agent has several things spinning around in their mind at the same time, while trying to tactfully deal with customers, improve their selling skill and closing ratio, and meet all demands for success at the end of the day! This tangled up "mental mess" roadblocks the enjoyment of conducting business on ANY level.

Nobody wins when you can't enjoy what you do. A scheduled day that offers specific chunks times to handle each and every daily duty in order, will separate the good, the bad, and the indifferent parts of your life, so that you are not mentally dealing with them all at once. The freedom this creates in your mind while you are selling is simply indescribable.

Everybody wins when you enjoy what you do. Without stressors mentally pressing you at all times, the agent is able to relax and enjoy locating customers who have a need for final expense protection. This relaxed and cheerful disposition will transfer good vibes that a customer will pick up on. This generates value to people in need of coverage. Sales occur more often. Quality business is written. The client, agent, and insurance carrier all win together.

There is no doubt in my heart of hearts that a weekly selling schedule is a must for the successful final expense insurance agent.

View a sample Agent (Starter) Schedule on the following page to generate ideas about what your own agent weekly schedule should look like.

It is my approach to start by setting aside specific blocks of time for selling on Monday . Then insert around those blocks of **selling time**, all of life's *other* obligations and responsibilities, i.e.: errands, return phone calls, email, doctor/dentist visit, school functions, lunch and supper, paying bills, groceries, etc.

Then, do the same with Tuesday. Start with blocks of time for selling, and schedule *everything else* around your selling time. Same for Wednesday through Friday.

Although Saturday is an **excellent selling day** during the week, the following illustration chart does not include Saturday to be formatted to fit the page.

Live and die by your schedule! To maintain a profitable business every day, you must **discipline yourself** to see productive DAILY results (sales).

Presentation/Schedule/Diet/Faith 171

AGENT (STARTER) SCHEDULE

* FEPS = Final Expense Phone Sales.

	Mon	Tues	Wed	Thur	Fri
8am	Client Bday cards	Organize Phone Appts	Organize Phone Appts	Organize Phone Appts.	Organize next week Phn Appts
9am	FEPS	FEPS	FEPS	FEPS	FEPS
10am	FEPS	FEPS	FEPS	FEPS	FEPS
11am	FEPS	FEPS	FEPS	FEPS	FEPS
12pm	Lunch Email Return Calls	Lunch Email Return Calls	Lunch Email Return Calls	Lunch Email Return Calls	Lunch Email Return Calls
1pm	FEPS	FEPS	FEPS	FEPS	FEPS
2pm	FEPS	FEPS	FEPS	FEPS	FEPS
3pm	FEPS Workshop	FEPS	FEPS Workshop	FEPS	FEPS
4pm	Pay bills / Conserve Business / Mail	FEPS	Appts-Doc Mail / Pay bills /	FEPS	Appts-Doc Conserve Business / Mail
5pm	Supper Emails Return Calls	Supper Emails Return Calls	Supper Email Return Calls	Supper Emails Return Calls	Supper Email Return Calls
6pm	FEPS	FEPS	FEPS	FEPS	FEPS
7pm	FEPS	FEPS	FEPS	FEPS	FEPS
8pm	FEPS	FEPS	FEPS	FEPS	FEPS
9pm	Stop	Stop	Stop	Stop	Stop

I have learned that it is best for me to not read any emails, not listen to any phone messages, not to read or answer mail, or access the daily news before making my first sale of the day. Since I used to do all of these in the morning first thing, my schedule changed for **when** I do all of these.

I want to give no one the chance to put something negative into my mind that would dampen my spirit first thing in the morning. This may sound silly, but I make sales quicker and EASIER with a 100% positive, mental disposition. I pay attention to what negatively affects my selling "mojo", and eliminate it, or divert it somehow.

Each morning, I begin dialing, talking, presenting, and serving policies, with a fresh mind. It does make a huge difference to me. I want to succeed to the point that I put into practice whatever ethically works, even if it means making a new and different lifestyle choice, so that my schedule wins the bottom-line profit I desire to earn at the close of each and every week.

MY SCHEDULE IS MY BOSS.

Because I am a self employed insurance professional, it is tempting for family and friends to expect me to drop what I am doing at any time of the day to lend assistance to their cause or need.

Moving furniture, transportation for a doctor appointment, paying bills, social functions, sporting events, hospital sitting, etc., all of these favors for others who we love is noble, but can also easily take a final expense agent without a weekly schedule out of the selling seat. At the end of the week, you have helped everyone else, except your broke self.

Allowing my family, friends, and business associates to know that I work from a weekly schedule is the best way to be insulated from their intruding expectations. In the words of one of my own agents, *"It is amazing how something so simple (a weekly schedule) can be so liberating!"*

My close family, friends, and business associates know when I will be returning phone calls, when I answer email, and when I can and cannot entertain personal visits. My agent weekly schedule earns their respect to not infringe on my valuable selling time.

Suppose I worked on an assembly line in a factory. I punch a time clock to begin working. In the middle of the afternoon my cousin calls my cell phone to ask me to help him move a pool table into his basement. I tell my cousin I'll have to check with my supervisor. The boss says, *"Are you crazy? If you want to keep you job, you'd better keep working on that assembly line. No."*

Presentation/Schedule/Diet/Faith

As a self employed insurance agent, you are BOTH employ**er** and employ**ee**. A supervisor in a factory sets quotas - daily production results. If production falls behind in your area of labor for 2-3-4-5 days in a row, you'll get fired. A self employed business professional applies this concept to his daily schedule and demands from himself daily production results that normally a supervisor would. An average insurance agent without this discipline or self accountability is, in effect, firing himself. Who is your **real** boss? Is it your schedule?

If someone asks you to take time away from selling insurance, check with your boss – your Agent Weekly Schedule. If your schedule says you should be doing telesales at that particular time, the answer is, *"Sorry, did you know that I have a schedule that I work by? It will have to wait until after 5pm."*

When people ask for favors from you, the agent, let them know, *"Hey, did you know that I work from a weekly schedule now?"* Sensible people will respect this structure in your business, especially if they notice your success!

The business associates in my office all have a copy of my weekly schedule. I have made all of them aware of how to take phone messages for me, how to handle personal visits for me, and how to notify me in case of a family crisis emergency.

No wonder I enjoy final expense phone sales! When I am in my office selling and serving insurance policies, I am insulated and protected from negatory stressors, as well as tempting distractions, within my Agent Weekly Schedule.

To be a consistent producer with policies being sold daily, it requires 1000% focus. Having an initial desire to succeed is only half of an accurate focus.

The other half of complete focus is working a plan (Agent Weekly Schedule). An agent simply must not allow life's other "good" distractions to overlap selling time. An Agent Weekly Schedule keeps the focus right on what brings profitable results at week's end.

Some examples of life's realities and choices that will take an agent away from the selling seat are: day stock trading, errand running, a side business, volunteer work, children and family requests, fixing the washing machine, helping people move, paying bills, care giving to the sick, or writing a book (ha ha)!

Diet and Final Expense

Many aspects of an agent's personal life can contribute to profitably selling final expense insurance. One overlooked area is your physical health.

Some of this cannot be controlled. Much of it, in my humble and professional opinion, we can control. So, how does your physical health connect to making sales sooner than not?

P-s-s-s-t..*We really are what we eat.*

What you eat has a lot to do with how you feel. How you feel translates to the customer how they perceive you over the telephone. How a customer perceives you over the telephone has **everything** to do with *whether or not you make a sale.*

If you **sound** unhappy or tired over the telephone, a customer will not take much confidence in what you are offering to them. Your every word, every voice inflection, is being read like a book by the customer!

One's diet, therefore, actual connects to an agent's increased ability or inability to make sales in this respect. If you feel good, a customer can actual tell it, even over the telephone. If you feel lousy, a customer can pick up on that, too. A customer will sooner gravitate toward an upbeat, positive, joyful person.

It can't be faked. An agent who thinks how they truly feel can be hidden from the customer is only fooling himself. You must be for real. This is why I pay attention to my diet. To me, it is worth observing and improving every area within myself, if it will give me an edge to making sales sooner.

Proper eating and sleeping today and tonight is VITAL to how a person feels tomorrow.

Especially during winter months, I highly recommend a healthy, diet that boosts your own immune system. I rarely get sick, while our fast food-n-artificial beverage nation languishes in colds, the latest flu, viruses, allergies, or even worse – the runny nose!

3 cans of soda have enough sugar in them to shut down a healthy person's immune system for 24 hours. My beverage of choice during the day is distilled water, or a juice beverage.

Caffeine ingested within the human body is a potent toxin that neutralizes the immune system, not boosting it. The main reason why coffee lends "energy" is because the immune system kicks into hyper-drive with an adrenaline release, trying to usher this toxic poison to the nearest exit before it reaches cellular level. The after-effect of ingesting caffeine is tiredness, because your body has worked overtime to get it all out of your system.

I consume high energy "living" foods for lunch. Salads! Green leafy vegetables are chocked full of living enzymatic life (powerful building blocks on the cellular level). I never, EVER eat fast foods consisting of white breads, or heavy foods for lunch, such as: pasta, red meats, dairy, etc.

My snack of choice is granola or a fruit bar, not candy bars, or pastry. I **NEVER** get the "afternoon lull", or the mid day "sleepy syndrome", rather, I make sales!

Ever feel the 1-4pm nap coming on? When a person feels sluggish mid afternoon, it is often because their blood-flow and living enzyme nutrients are gravitating to the digestive area of the stomach to process and breakdown thick, heavy foods consumed at the noon meal. Bodily energy literally goes south.

This takes blood flow away from the brain, resulting in light-headed, wheezy slumber.

My energy level and mental alertness remains just as high at mid afternoon as it is in the morning. Why?

Fresh fruits, vegetables, and nuts (almonds, cashews, walnuts, and pecans) are a living source of enzymatic life as antioxidants, nutrients, vitamins, and trace minerals boost your body's ability to combat sickness or tiredness throughout the day.

In my world of successful selling, this is **equally as important** to having a great sales script. If I *feel* good, I sell good. Period.

I rise early in the morning (5-6am) like a race horse at the starting gate, because I go to bed at a reasonably early hour. I normally arrive at my office between 7-8am. Plenty of deep sleep (approx. 8 hrs.) allows the body enough time to fully cleanse, rejuvenate, and replenish bacteria-fighting strength.

From the crown of my head to the sole of my feet, I believe with every fiber of my being that this is a direct benefit to making daily sales. I also believe that my healthy diet has elevated me to become a more consistently effective salesperson.

It all boils down to this. Ask yourself, the next time you swallow that Honey Bun, *"How does this food help me to make a sale today?"* If what you are eating and poor sleep habits make you tired, and prone to sickness by weakening your immune system, it takes you out of the selling seat.

Does it sound smart to you to allow unhealthy foods and beverages to continue having access to your body?

I don't think so.

Faith and Final Expense

WORK
like everything depends on you.
PRAY
like everything depends on God.

It is my humble opinion that there is a miraculous element within every sale. A policy sold is the intricate combining of two worlds - the customer's and the agent's.
How one sale all comes together, to me, is providential. Yet, I never use my faith as a crutch to sell a policy, or to make a spiritual appeal to a religious customer.
Expressing a testimony of faith by an agent initially may buy a religious customer's interest up front, but can easily backfire on the agent at the close. A religious customer avoiding a buying decision today expects a religious agent to simply "understand" if they need to "pray about it", even though this is NOT a *spiritual* decision.
"Pray about it" simply means we want more time to ultimately say "no thanks". It is the same with all customers, both non-religious and religious alike - final expense protection is an important decision **today**. It is not important tomorrow, especially if the customer has no coverage.
I would rather a final expense customer respect me because I am a professional agent, not because I am a Christian. It matters at the close.
At the dawn of each selling day, I say a little prayer. I ask for Divine assistance to be led to the right customer who is also looking just for my professional assistance with burial expense protection today.
Here is a sample prayer that I make to my Heavenly Father before each day of serving final expense plans to the general public:

> *Heavenly Father,*
> *Help me to cross the path of those who need*
> *my help with final expense protection today.*
> *Lead me away from those who want to waste my*
> *time, or who are not interested in my service.*
> *I want to make a real friend today,*
> *and protect a family's future.*
> *Take me to the one who*
> *needs what I have to*
> *offer now.*
> *Amen.*

Only <u>after a policy is sold</u> will I share with a religious client, my daily prayer of direction, and that I believe it was no accident that we are on the telephone together.

My Job / God's Job Principle

How do God and I partner together in business? Do I, a National Top Producer, really require assistance from above? Is one, successful sale within my control alone? Hardly.

All the stars and planets have to 'line up perfectly" – a lot of things must fall exactly into place - just to be able to make one sale. Truth is, several of these key factors are outside of my control.

The difference between me and a lot of other experts is that I am willing to admit that my success, one sale at a time, is not all about me.

The greatest kept secret of enjoying successful selling is to accept Heaven's help. I'll take all the Divine assistance I can get !

The Holy Bible says, *"The blessing of the LORD, it maketh rich, and he addeth no sorrow with it"* (Proverbs 10:22).

These words were penned by the richest man in history, Israel's King Solomon, whose legendary wisdom still confounds us three millennia later.

It is estimated, by the detailed architectural design and lavish building materials laid out in the book of II Chronicles, that the Temple of Worship built by Solomon was worth by today's standards, a whopping 174 **billion** dollars!

We have nothing on our planet to compare it to. Bill Gates' 200 **m**illion dollar mansion would look like the outhouse to King Solomon's Temple. It would be safe to say that King Solomon probably knew a thing or two about acquiring then wisely handling joyous wealth that we should learn a thing or two from, eh?

Because my relationship to God is an important part of my life, I try not to do God's job for Him. I give to God oversight of the results in my business. If He is in charge of the universe, can't He orchestrate putting me together with customers who need my help today?

Again, the Divinely inspired Proverb mentioned previously, states that blessings (sales) that are of the Lord's doings will be quality business (...*he addeth no sorrow with it.*). Sorrow, or regret, is attached to wealth earned in the wrong way, through unethical techniques, or at the wrong time (too fast).

God created and loves me, although I am not perfect. He wants me to be fulfilled, happy, and successful in the purpose of my existence. His purpose for me is not failure.

It is a part of mature, adult growth to let go of success based on dollars, and instead become motivated by success based on becoming a better man in His plan. There is a Scriptural guarantee in Proverbs 10:22 that my life will be rich in blessings without any regrets, as a direct benefit in God's Plan for my life.

So, what is the plan?

First of all, God does His job, as bound by His Word. I also have a certain job of responsibility, as articulated in the Word of God.

What is God's job? What is my job?

The answer lies in the Holy Scripture, another proverb of King Solomon, Proverbs 3:6. There are 12 words in this verse. *"In all thy ways acknowledge him (God), and he (God) shall direct thy path."*

The first 6 words are my job – *"In all thy ways acknowledge him..."*. It is my job to acknowledge God. It is my job to put Him on the throne of my heart every day. It is my job to honor Him. It my job to magnify Him. It is my job to please God, in everything I am and do, including selling final expense insurance. My life is to honor God in my work ethic and business practice. That's my job.

I have miserably failed in my life at times to do my job. Yet, God is a Master Designer of the second chance. I have learned the hard way that life works out best the better I fulfill my job in acknowledging and honoring my Creator-God in all that I do or say.

The remaining 6 words in Proverbs 3:6 are God's job, *"...and he shall direct thy path."* As I am focused on accomplishing my job, it is then God's job to direct me. It is His job to cross my path with someone who desperately needs help with funeral and burial protection today, as I am doing my job.

You see, I have zero control over what is happening on the opposite end of the telephone. So, I simply focus on performing my job of making sales presentations in a way and work ethic that would please my Creator- God.

I cannot create a need for my product on the customer's end. God does. He is orchestrating the daily events in the lives of my customers.

It is also God's job to guide me around those not really interested, or people who want to jerk my chain, or people who do not need what I have to offer, so that I may get to the person who does need my professional assistance sooner today than later.

All of this that God does on my behalf may, in fact, be unseen. I do not notice behind the scenes what is being accomplished by God on the customer's side. My Divine Partner follows through on His end of the deal, as bounds by the contract of His Holy Scripture to handle the results, as I am fulfilling my job.

It is my Creator who props the customer's situation to require my professional assistance. It is also my Creator who puts me together and in front of needy people who appreciate the opportunity to receive what I have to offer, as I dial leads and make contact with prospective customers, IF MY WORK ETHIC HONORS GOD (my job).

This is God and I working our business in tandem. We join together for blessings (sales) earned the right way having no regrettable reprisals (sorrow) added to it.

This "My Job/God's Job" principle applies to every single aspect of my final expense insurance business. It is ultimately God's job to handle the results of my mailer response rates, contract points, commissions paid, cancelled policies, promotions, client circumstances, and SALES. I only focus on doing well what I can control – serving final expense insurance in a work ethic that honors Him.

I **do not** try to do God's job for Him. I do not try to manipulate the outcome of results. I never try to calculate the next sale by crunching numbers, or figuring dials to contacts to presentations ratios. This creates undue stress and worry. That is, I leave every aspect of business **results,** which I have no control over, into the capable hands of my God, Who loves me and desires the best success for me, because I accurately acknowledge HIM in my business.

This liberates me to not worry about the results that I cannot control, which is God's job.

There are two captions I see on my desk every morning. One is written on a 3x5 card directly in my line of sight while engaged in sales:

> **KEEP YOUR ATTITUDE RIGHT**
> **STAY FOCUSED**
> **STAY POSITIVE**
> **TRUST IN THE LORD.**

Another caption inside a picture frame is located on the shelf above my desk.

> **And he said,**
> **The things which are impossible**
> **with men**
> **are possible with God.**
> **Luke 18:27**

These two inspirational captions lend moment-by-moment guidance in the delicate course of selling's ups and downs. I need reminders that put my mind and heart at ease when things do not go my way or according to "my plan".

In my world, there is a Higher Power that engineers all circumstances to the final result of what is good for me.

God created and loves me.

What I think is good for me today, may not be best for me today. So, I work smart, trusting in a loving God to do His job of overseeing business results. This keeps my disposition positive and healthy, because He is ALWAYS in control.

God does not fail. If I follow His Scriptural plan for my life, neither will I.

Blaming God for Failure

All too often, non-productive agents, who unfortunately also claim to be Christian, inaccurately "spiritualize" their own failures.

By this I mean, an agent averaging only 1-3 sales per week, because of laziness, or inactivity on the phone, or an unwillingness to apply advice from their manager, will announce, *"It must not be God's Will for me to do telesales"*, or *"If God doesn't 'do something' in the next week or two to boost my production, I'm outta' here"*, or *"God better help me out soon, if He wants me to keep doing this."*

Tisk, tisk. How dare an agent blame God for their failure to improve **him/herself**, work hard, and forsake a losing attitude!

God is a gracious Friend Who blessed you with an opportunity to employ yourself each and every day while much of our country languishes in job famine.

If you, a licensed insurance agent within our organization, are not fully accessing and maximizing the free-flowing telesales system in front of you, the selling advice and FREE coaching sessions from Top Producers, as well as learning to increase selling skills from your own trial-and-error experience, shame on you! If your backside is not in the selling seat during normal working hours of a regular job, shame on you double!! If you are more distracted by trivial fun, or "doing other things", and are not focusing 1000% on doing telesales in a productive manner, than feeding your family with a comfortable income, I feel sorry for you in eternity when God asks you why His answer to your prayers for a lucrative income in final expense sales was not good enough for you to give your best to.

God is not obligated to "bail out" an agent who is not getting the job done on his end! God helps those who help themselves.

Truth is, if any agent within our organization is not working 6-8 hours on the telephone per day nonstop (except for lunch and 15 min. breaks in mid morning and afternoon), not dialing nonstop, not talking nonstop, not presenting nonstop, until the agent makes one sale today, then let's put the blame where it really belongs, and not on God's "inability" to "make something happen".

On the flip side, if an agent works a solid 8 hour day on the telephone, making 5-7 full presentations today in the right way without seeing results at the close of one day, this agent can hold his head up high. There is no shame in striking out in valiant effort. I strike out once in a while myself, but you better believe if I strike out, it was not because I was "cherry picking" leads, dialing sporadically during a few menial hours of effort, or toying with sideline amusements, then announce, *"God better make something happen soon."*

Get real! God has already answered your prayers for financial growth by giving to you the great privilege and golden opportunity to earn a six figure income working smart 5 days every single week from your own office. It is not up to God to do any more than that. Employ yourself! Apply yourself!! Improve yourself!!!

If an agent fails to make sales, due to inactivity (less than 7-8 SOLID HOURS) on the telephone 5 consecutive days per week, then take God off trial.

The Creator is an "equal opportunity rewarder". He helps those who help themselves. To find most of the reason why your personal production is slack, go look into the mirror before blaming God!

Can you tell that blaming God for failure is a "pet peeve" of mine?

Parental Final Expense Responsibility

Once in a while, I have the misfortune to listen to a thick-headed, or misguided customer in their sunset years of life, drone on and on about justifying their non-decision to do something about taking care of inevitable end-of-life future expenses, because - *"I have done s-o-o-o much for my children. Now, it is time for them to take care of me when I die"*.

Even worse, a shortsighted, religious customer may throw God's Word into the mix, stating the Scripture verse that says, *"Children honor your parents for this is right..."*.

Of course, coming from a theological background of Bible degrees, having grown up in a minister's home myself, and delivering scores of Biblical messages, I know that this verse is being completely taken out of its scriptural context and being turned over on its head by the customer.

At any rate, if a customer inaccurately uses God as a crutch for justifying a poor decision to not protect their family from financial hardship, because of a lack of individual responsibility as a parent, I direct these type customers to a certain Scripture verse that puts end-of-life responsibility where it belongs within a parent/child relationship.

The Apostle Paul wrote several instructional letters under Divine Inspiration to the early New Testament churches of Asia Minor between 35 and 50 A.D. These divinely inspired letters later came together to form one-third of the Holy Bible's inspired New Testament. (See my book *"The Perfect Bible"* at **TroyClark.net**)

Paul was known immediately after Christ's death for having "care of all the churches", meeting head on certain falsehoods that crept into the New Testament early churches of Asia Minor, as they were developing from their spiritual infancy into doctrinal maturity.

Before his third missionary journey to the church at Corinth, Paul's letter preceding his arrival reveals where financial obligations rest between parents and their adult children.

II Corinthians 12:14
Behold, the third time I am ready to come to you;
and I will not be burdensome to you...
for the children ought not to lay up for the parents,
but the parents for the children.

I recall actually asking customers who have a Bible handy to turn to this passage and read it for themselves. It plainly states a *parental* duty to "lay up", or to "reserve financially" for future costs, against that which would negatively impact a family's future, NOT the other way around, as a duty of *children*.

In proper context, Paul sets the example by stating his own reluctance to place any kind of a "financial burden" on his "spiritual children" of the faith in this particular church. For children, says Paul by Divine authority, ought not to have to secure financial arrangements for their parents under normal circumstances.

Principally, this applies to the financial means in taking care of one's final expenses. It rests squarely on an *individual responsibility of the parent*, and is **not** a "corporate responsibility" placed upon the entire family or adult children. To claim otherwise does not square with God's Holy Scripture and is backward to correct thinking.

It is hard for a Bible believing Christian to bypass what Holy Scripture plainly says after reviewing this verse. I have sold policies to Christian clients based on this powerful Scripture verse.

Once we establish who is Scripturally responsible to put financial reserves in place within a religious parent-child relationship, final expense insurance makes more sense to the parent.

Scriptural Guide To Productivity Results

He which **soweth sparingly** shall **reap** also **sparingly**; and he which **soweth bountifully** shall **reap** also **bountifully**.

II Corinthians 9:6

It is a universal law. Many begins with one. Yet, one came from previous many.

Many sales come one at a time. Yet, one sale came from many previous attempts.

Without getting too deep for my own little pea brain, I am only relating how one big goal (financial success) is made up of many smaller goals (dials, presentations, sales per day, per week).

The agent who puts in consecutive hours on the telephone is going to have more production to show at week's end than the agent who hits-and-misses an hour here, an hour there, on the telephone.

You only reap what you sow.

The Holy Bible makes it very clear. The greatest harvest goes to a faithfully fulfilled work schedule. Any activity apart from the final expense sales telephone, during selling hours, will render sparse financial gain.

To benefit the most on our telesales platform, an expert telesales agent must labor in the sales field. This is ENJOYABLE WORK if done in the right way.

The way I see it, on Monday morning I start "scattering seed" by dialing lead contacts, leaving voice messages to those who do not answer, and schedule appointments for married couples. By Monday afternoon and Tuesday, I have several return phone messages, appointments set, and sprouts of potential growth toward personal production.

This requires hours of steady "seed spreading" in the earliest part of the week. By Tuesday afternoon, there are more people to call back and make presentations to than I can possibly work into my weekly schedule.

I can then become selective in the harvest process of making sales. Some lead contacts leave a message by returning my earlier call. These customers may have a sense of urgency in their voice for me to call with benefit information. Other voice messages by interested customers reveal a minor curiosity.

Nevertheless, the more phone call seeds I sow, the more I get to pick and choose which customers I spend my time with during prime selling hours Monday through Friday.

There is absolutely no reaping without the sowing. Mark it down.

In addition, the amount of reaping (making sales) is in direct proportion to the amount of sowing (dialing, talking, presenting) employed by an individual agent.

Because I did not understand everything about telesales at first, I poured in 65 hours my first full week on the telephone. I generated 9 sales by week's end by simply stacking the odds in my favor with a tremendous number of **imperfect** sales presentations, hours worked, and incalculable numbers of dials.

Most agents marvel over hearing about 9 sales my full week of selling final expense insurance over the telephone. What is ignored is the fact that when you divide 9 sales into 65 hours, that equals 1 policy sold *every 7 hours on the telephone.* How many policies would I have sold if I only worked 20-30 hours my first week?

There is no secret pill or magic wand to successful results in selling. It is simply work, consistent, principled, smart WORK.

Only God is Great

Troy Clark in himself is not a great man. I am a natural born sinner whose soul has been saved by Jesus Christ by asking for salvation in a simple prayer of faith.

The greatest accomplishment and happiest moment in my entire life occurred on April 14, 1973, when I understood God's simple plan of salvation, and received God the Son into my heart and life as a personal Savior.

Look not to any earthly awards I have achieved as great. Look only to my Heavenly King. He creates, sustains, saves, recovers, and blesses all life. My insurance career, and any success that I have earned by it, is only meant to be a light to point you to Him.

It would be foolish of me to not give kudos to the Great Architect of Life and Conqueror over death, hell, and sin.

Is it foolish to believe in God? A definition of a fool is *"one who makes adequate preparation for this life, but who makes **no preparation** for the life to come."*

Confidence in successfully serving final expense insurance is led by a personal assurance that your own end-of-life protection is cared for.

My end-of-life **eternal** coverage is all taken care of by God. My end-of-life **earthly** coverage is all squared away as well with final expense insurance.

Both ways, I'm covered!

If you prefer to not believe that there is a God in Heaven who seeks to Love You as you are right now, don't you at least wish you could? It does not really matter if you do not believe in God. He still believes in You.

Trusting in His Word is the most important decision in this life you could ever make. To arrive in Heaven after you leave this life, believe on the Lord Jesus Christ.

For God so loved the world, that he gave his only begotten Son, that whosoever believeth in him should not perish, but have everlasting life. John 3:16

Most people want God to bless their plan. Reverse it.
YOU get in on God's Plan:

Prayer of Salvation:
Dear God, I understand that I am a sinner. I understand that Jesus died on the cross to pay for my sins, so that I would not have to go to hell and pay for my own sins. I understand Jesus is the only way to Heaven, according to your Holy Word. Dear Jesus, please forgive my sins. Please, come into my heart and save my soul. I am trusting in you. Thank you for your forgiveness and love for me. Amen.

Only God is great !

Chapter Five

Agent Pitfalls
Straight Talk on Selling
Can-Do Spirit

*Achievers look for reasons to succeed.
Critics look for reasons to fail.
Which one have you become?*

Troy Clark

Agent Pitfalls in Selling Final Expense

Caller Reluctance

Caller reluctance is the dark side of professional selling. It is also referred to as "Phone Phobia."

To borrow a military phrase, caller reluctance is a form of "shell shock". Shell shock in insurance comes from a perceived negative outcome, whether imaginary or by a real-life experience, to the agent:

- Rejection by a customer.
- Afraid of the unknown.
- A new learning curve in sales.
- Dumbfounded over hang-ups by customers.
- Overwhelmed by life's personal issues.
- Feelings of inadequacy.
- Being yelled at on the phone by the callee.
- Don't know why. Just do not want to call.

From motivational czar Zig Ziglar to university case studies, it is reported that 40-80% of all sales professionals experience caller reluctance to the point of threatening their selling career. I, Troy Clark, am no exception.

Rookies have it. Pros have it. Sales managers pass it along to their agents. If you stay overwhelmed by caller reluctance, you're not just wasting time, you're losing money. And, you stand in jeopardy of killing your insurance sales career.

Remember you are in charge of your own success as an Independent Business Owner. So take the dreams of your future into your own hands. Learn how to become a Master Sales Agent in this one area, and success will be yours.

The phenomenon of call reluctance is an inner personal experience by an elevated level of apprehension, often overwhelming, that may inhibit the number of calls a salesperson will make, and perhaps, rendering an individual agent incapable of working at all.

The telephone just looks like an elephant. It loathes the agent to pick it up and dial. Caller reluctance mocks the agent, causing a feeling of "I should be able to shake this. What's wrong with me?"
Caller reluctance at its ugliest renders a final expense sales agent useless.
Clearly, an Independent Business Owner has to be a self starter. Yet, a salesperson's ability to keep their emotions in check is also critically important. Being able to shove away from the dock of familiarity, and launch into a new business opportunity, has as much to do with being able to weather the storms of doubt that arise at some point in every person's professional career.

Understanding the problem is half the solution.

10 Signs of Caller Reluctance are symptoms that identify what is going on within an agent:

1. **Naysayer**: Worries. Will not take social risks to meet new people.
2. **Over Preparer**: Over analyzes. Under acts.
3. **Image Pro**: Obsessed with looking good. Average in presentation skills. Confuses promotional packaging with selling substance.
4. **Role Rejection**: Secretly ashamed of sales career. Deflects their own identity.
5. **Yielder**: Fears intruding on others.
6. **Self Conscious**: Intimidated by up-scale customers.
7. **Separatist**: Won't mix business with friends.
8. **Emotionless**: Unwilling to see another person's needs are as important as your own.
9. **Referral Aversion**: Fears ongoing business or client relationships.
10. **Opposition Reflex:** Argues, rebuffs, "talks over" others instinctively. Believes their opinion is always superior.

The stereotypical image of salespeople as over-socializing, fearless mercenaries of business is an image no sales expert wants to personify. Salespeople are asked to walk a fine line in our society.

Agent Pitfalls/Straight Talk/Can-Do Spirit

Our American culture is all too ready to conclude that excessive self promotion is "uncool". Yet, salespeople must engage in self promotion through business opportunities within appropriate limits. Successful sales experts have to learn to deal with this societal contradiction.

Caller reluctance arises through a basic fear over rejection, even alienation, or a fear of engaging in self promotion. A number of conditional fears may express themselves by any number of beliefs, diverse attitudes, past traumas, or array of behaviors and personal habits. Various dynamics can impact a selling situation.

In my humble opinion, caller reluctance is usually the result of (or an anxiousness caused by) focusing on something you have no control over.

It is wrapped up in the angst of trying to predict the unpredictable.

Will I get blessed out over calling someone who was napping? Will I skip any pages of the sales script? Will I make sense? Will someone buy a policy from me? What if I give the customer the wrong information? Does this selling system really work? What if the customer does not want to volunteer information that I need to process an application? What if, what if, what if....

Or, an agent may feel angst over something unrelated to selling.

*How am I going to pay the mechanic who is working on my vehicle if I do not make a sale? What if I am in the middle of a sale when my 4pm dentist appointment arrives? Am I going to make a sale before I have to pick up the kids from school? How am I going to pay for divorce and attorneys fees? Am I ready for out of town relatives visiting tonight? What are the response rates of my mailer leads? Is the insurance company **really** paying me for the policies I sell?*

(*Note: In the section titled "Agent Schedule", I address my caller reluctance over 'getting everything done' in the course of one day, one week. My Agent Weekly Schedule took care of when to handle every one of life's responsibilities, obligations, and all of life's 'unplanned realities'. I 'get it all done' in due course of my weekly schedule, so that I do not have a thousand different things spinning around in my head, while I am selling.

These stressors, and more, paralyze an agent. Self inflicted scenarios of doubt take over the reality of today's opportunity in the mind of an agent. An agent's focus at this point must be pivoted.

To release myself from caller reluctance, when it occurs, I focus on the positive things in my life that will continue, whether I make a sale or not. What are the positive things in your life that will remain the same whether you succeed or fail? Anchor there.

10 Solutions to Caller Reluctance that lends to an agent the framework to work your way out of apprehension and the darkness:

1. **Embrace Your Opportunity**: Caller reluctance gives an agent the golden opportunity to do something that most people in life never get the chance to do. IMPROVE YOURSELF. Although your life has hit the pause button, it nevertheless gives to the agent the ability to maximize what you can control – your growth. Out from past mediocrity is growing a personal transformation here. Embrace this as a gift !
2. **Thought Realignment**: Instead of focusing on what is outside of your control, find a specific element that you *enjoy* about final expense telesales, whether you make a sale or not. Allow this to become your reason for making calls. This is your anchor through tough moments. We all experience ups-n-downs in this business throughout each week. A focus stayed on the enjoyment aspect will keep you committed, sane, and balanced. It keeps you in control.
3. **Positive Reinforcement**: Realize that to every negative in life, there is a positive. Focus on the

sunny side. While others languish in a stalemate economy of unemployment, I have the unique privilege of employing myself. All that is required of me is to help people all day with their life insurance needs. How hard is that?
4. **Self Talk**: It is not events, either past or present, which make us feel the way we feel. Our feelings are caused by *what we tell ourselves* about our circumstances. Misguided, defeatist thoughts creep into the subconscious. Empower your reality instead! Say loudly, *"Average salespeople turn these situations into success to become Pros. If they can do it, I can do it. How do I turn this around into my advantage?" "I can do this." "This is going to be a great call". "I am going to have fun, whether the person I call is in a good mood or not."*
5. **Baby Steps.** Sometimes, it is as simple as calling 10 customers and say, *"Hi. My name is____. I am calling from ____. Here is my phone number to call, if your family is ever in need of any life insurance --- --- ----. Have a great day. Good bye."* Set a *doable* goal for yourself, even if it seems very small. Build upward from there.
6. **Desensitize the Threat**: Pressures of selling can seem unbearable in moments of franticness. Stand back. Take a deep breath. Detach yourself emotionally by recounting the many positive aspects of your life that will continue on regardless the outcome of the next call. The threat immediately becomes less dramatic.
7. **Thought Zapping**: This simple technique urges the agent to "get over it" when negative thoughts enter the mind. Sometimes it can be as simple as snapping a rubber band at the top of the wrist. Sometimes a splash of cold water to the face does the trick.
8. **Defeat the Real Enemy**: Assertive individuals enjoy a challenge over adversaries. Perhaps the goal of winning a long term business relationship

with a customer can be initially viewed in the short term as a challenge of 'winning' the customer's trust first. In focusing on 'defeating' the customer's initial reluctance, the agent has defeated the real enemy, his own caller reluctance.

9. **Plan for the Worst; Hope for the Best**: Plan beforehand what your reaction will be if you feel overwhelmed by the prospect of a person's rejection. I will say...."*Thank you for your time. Have a blessed day*", or "*I appreciate you expressing the truth about how you feel. I hope you feel better soon*", if a customer blows me off as uninterested, expresses aggravation over my call, or even shouts obscenities. Knowing what an agent's reaction will be ahead of time does not give power to the callee. Memorize a few easy lines of conversation that can be useful with any type of customer. No matter what happens, my response will respectfully be the same. This empowers the agent at all times and in all circumstances.

10. **Helpful Books**: Additional sources in books, articles, and online formats are available to an agent struggling with caller reluctance:

"Time Tactics of Very Successful People"(Griessman1994)
"The Fear Factor" (Fox 1992)
"Overcoming Sales-Call Reluctance" (Kadansky2001)
"The Dirty Little Secret" (Blackwood 1994)
"Let Your Life Speak" (Parker Palmer 2000)

Caller reluctance is **not** a character flaw. It is simply counterproductive thinking patterns or poor self-image thinking habits that disable agent confidence.

The best analogy of caller reluctance I know of is compared to entering into a swimming pool. Initially, there is apprehension over the cool temperature of the water. The person may even start to shiver before the water ever touches the skin, just because the person is looking at the water with predetermined thoughts of temperature clash.

Yet, most people agree, once the initial water-shock is overcome, it is over. Some people overcome the jolt of liquid coolness by wading in one toe at a time. Some people prefer a "cannonball" splash into the crisp blue.

From childhood, most adults know that the sooner the initial jar of temperature difference subsides, the sooner the water is enjoyed. The initial reluctance never goes away, however. It is always there, taunting us. However, through experience, it becomes easier and easier to manage the angst of what happens on the first attempt to make contact with the water.

However an agent chooses to overcome caller reluctance, the key is move forward. Nobody learns to swim, who stays in the plastic lounge chair.

SPQ Gold is an online evaluation to identify and fix the symptoms of sales caller reluctance.

Reach out for professional help, if you cannot figure out caller reluctance on your own. Successful agents do.

Come on in. The water is fine!!

The "Almost Sale".

If an agent is waiting on the perfect customer situation to work itself out in order to indeed make a sale today, it rarely happens. Easy sales are the result of a lot of previous hard work by a relentless agent.

Final expense sales opportunity does not promise greener pastures. What we do deliver is a guarantee for the best sales equipment, seed, irrigation system, and "sales land" for you to farm. The crop result in your sales field is up to your own individual efforts. We give you the opportunity to simply employ and apply yourself.

Because I was not born wealthy, or blessed with a lot of natural talent, it forces me to become driven toward personal goals of self improvement.

I am a thinker and a doer. I am a go-getter. Although I would prefer to be a casual observer, I do not sit back and watch things happen. I must make success happen, if I am to enjoy it. I believe this initiative has much to do with the sales level I have been fortunate enough to reach.

A lot of final expense agents are not self starters. A lot of self starters are not finishers.

The two hardest things in life to do are: **Starting** and **Finishing**. What happens in between really doesn't matter. What really matters is a good start, and to finish what you have started.

In my professional opinion, the "Almost Sale" is the most common pitfall of agents who have a strong desire to start, but a weakness to finish. The difference between winning and losing a sale today, is what is takes to detour you.

Success and failure are on the same road. Success is just a little bit farther down the road. It is better for an individual to decide to finish something, than it is to decide to start something.

Agents who are not focused on finishing will be lured off course by what I call the "Almost Sale".

Suppose an agent has a customer on the phone who desires coverage. They desperately need coverage. It is 10am. The customer expresses their gratefulness for your call and has also expressed their sure desire to get coverage with you, the agent, today. However, the customer is elderly and needs to have an adult daughter with her to help her pick out one of the final expense plans. The daughter's arrival to the customer's home will be 3pm when the daughter is off work. The elderly customer insists that if you call her back at 3pm, the sale is good as made today.

QUESTION: What would you do?

A short-sighted agent will be fooled into thinking this sale is a sure thing. I can tell you from experience, it is not. Suppose the agent stops working, stops dialing, stops calling leads, stops making presentations, because the agent is banking on the customer's situation to work out *later* in order to make a sale today.

BIG MISTAKE.

Between 10am-3pm the agent runs errands, pays bills, surfs the internet, makes day trades on the stock market, ad infinity...then places a return call to the client at 3pm expecting the perfect situation to be in place to make a sale. No answer.

The truth is, I have a stack of leads printed out about 5 inches high, scores of them, piled up like old bundles of newspapers, of sure customer sales that were "almost" made, minus one small detail that never worked out. Had I based my insurance career on these "almost sales", I would not be writing this book today.

Can you think of a perfect sales situation that turned out later to be dud?

Here is an example list of "Almost Sales":

- A customer needs and wants coverage now. Has a doctor appointment now. Will be home mid afternoon. Call me later! No answer.
- A spouse wants immediate coverage at 11am, but the other spouse is at work. Call after 5pm to cover both. No answer.
- An agent who only calls previous clients for promised referrals, instead of dialing through "B" or "C" leads.
- A customer has no bank account, but will open one up immediately to get coverage, then call the agent back today. Customer never calls back.
- Early morning, a customer suggests an agent call back at 12 o'clock lunch. A decision will be reached by then to take coverage. The agent gets the customer's answer machine the rest of the day.
- An agent's inactivity on the phone, until more "A" leads arrive, because the agent mistakenly thinks the newest leads have more sure buyers in them.
- A customer chooses a plan. The sale is made. Cannot give bank information, until a family member arrives later in the day with the checkbook. Call after 4pm. No answer.

An expert agent learns to spot the "Almost Sale" and never relies on it. When a customer's situation does not initial work out to take coverage immediately, reschedule the appointment for sure.

However, KEEP WORKING, and talking, and presenting to other people. Do not stop dialing. Never stop working if a "sure" sale is not completely finished! If you stop to break when you think you've made a sale, without really making a sale, you are simply holding up your own progress.

Top Producers do the best with what they've got. No one has perfect situations to work with every time, every day. You must make success happen with the time, resources, and opportunity that you have access to right now.

An agent should not rely on another person's life to work out, to make a sale today.

Rely on yourself!

Focus only on what you can control. Never put your focus on what you have no control over. Can you control what a customer does who lives hundreds of miles away from you?

An "Almost Sale" is not a sale.

What you can control is your ability to dial, talk, and present a coverage plan to the "next person in line" who will give you the time of day over the phone. Keep working. Never celebrate too early.

This is how to make a minimum of one or more sales per day, and a six figure annual income after all business expenses are paid. This is what it takes to master final expense.

Suppose an agent correctly keeps working in between the initial call to the elderly customer and the rescheduled follow up call later in the afternoon. A sale is made, because the agent kept working in spite of the pending "Almost Sale".

Now, for the rescheduled follow up call, the elderly customer now has her daughter with her at 3pm. The

appointment can now proceed forward. Final expense coverage is served. Another sale is made. Two sales in one day are always better than one, eh? If the elderly customer and her daughter did not sign up for any coverage, **the agent still made one sale today!**
Did you *start* to make a sale today? Did you *finish* making sales today?

If an agent is not dialing one call right after the next, then this agent does not understand what it takes to be successful in final expense phone sales.

If you, the final expense agent, make a career choice of selling final expense insurance over the telephone successfully, then talking on the telephone is a necessity to make telesales.

Inactivity on the phone is your biggest threat to success.

An agent must be on the phone during ALL hours of a normal workday to see sales results.

Maybe it goes without saying. Maybe not. How many phone calls do I answer while doing final expense telesales? NONE. (Phone messages are listened to and phone calls are returned within my daily schedule, not during selling time) How many emails do I answer while doing final expense phone sales? NONE. (My email is not even open) How many knocks at the door do I answer while doing final expense phone sales? NONE (I lock the front door!)

Unless it is a family crisis emergency, NOTHING (and I mean nothing) is allowed to distract my selling time. Absolutely Nothing.

If World War III erupted while I am doing telesales, I would not know it, until the next scheduled break within my daily schedule. If the next "9/11" happened in my own city, I would not know it, until the next scheduled break within my daily schedule. Get the picture here?

This is what "working smarter" means. It takes no talent, no skill, no natural ability, and no higher education to own a high level of commitment to telesales within a daily/weekly schedule.

Because I have no interferences while doing my telesales, I can focus only on making dial after dial on the telephone, until I cross paths with a buyer. This helps me to make a sale sooner than later in the day. The sooner I can make a sale, the sooner I can make the next sale.

If you keep a snowball rolling, it adds more growth. If you stop rolling the snowball, what happens? No growth. Sales growth occurs as an agent keeps dialing, talking, and presenting.

An agent who is actually *not* on the phone dialing leads and making presentations, while supposedly "doing telesales", is encumbered by such distractions as paperwork, internet news, emails, office chatter, family, phone calls, visits from anyone, stock trading, tracking lead response rates, pouring over policy cancellations/declines, etc. etc. etc.

This only prolongs an agent's daily success.

Rookie agents become enamored by the "Almost Sale". It is a powerful and tempting prospect to believe that a sure sale is "going to happen" later. It is a more realistic, hard lesson to learn that a "sure" thing does not happen always, unless you move on to make other sales with other customers. This means finishing what you started today in telesales.

If you, a final expense sales professional, stop working, because you think a sure sale will be made later on today – you sadly are still a rookie.

TOP PRODUCERS never stop working, dialing, talking, presenting, and selling, until a sale is made TODAY.

Emotional Investment

A final expense insurance agent must be careful not to set yourself up for constant disappointment.

An agent will be meeting and talking to many potential clients in the course of one day, if the agent is working a professional schedule.

People have real life needs and traumas. A caring person, such as myself, must decide how to handle each

Agent Pitfalls/Straight Talk/Can-Do Spirit

customer situation wisely. It is not good, however, for an agent to empathetically invest him/herself emotionally with a customer up front. Guard your own heart. You do not owe anything to a customer who sent in a lead card, except for one conversation about funeral and burial protection benefits. Be warm upfront, but not overzealously "cozy" with a customer.

It is easier for an agent to go onto the next lead and keep dialing after you are turned down by a customer, or treated rudely, or cannot qualify a well-meaning individual, if you did not invest a lot emotionally in them to begin with.

Avoid inquiring into a customer's personal life problems. Listen to a customer who volunteers information about themselves, or a troubling situation. Yet, an agent should not seek to counsel customers. This is not your job.

Unwise agents entertain deep conversations about personal problems with customers, thinking that they are winning the customer's trust to make a sale in the end. Wrong. In the end, the customer will be more likely to stall coverage on themselves, because their excuse will inevitably have something to do with the personal problem the agent already "understands".

One way to pivot a conversation back to final expense coverage is for an agent to listen respectfully to a customer problem unrelated to funeral coverage, then say:

"I am sorry this happened to you. Thank you for sharing a little bit about yourself with me. You have a lot of concerns on your mind. I am able to help you with one of them today. **Tell me, what are your thoughts and concerns about your family when you sent the card back to me for our benefits available here***?"*

The bottom line is this. Only begin to invest yourself emotionally with a customer after they have expressed a specific need for funeral and burial protection and a desire for your professional assistance to fill their need. Then, and only then, my heart joins in.

Out of Focus

On a final expense sales platform, what ***you choose not to do*** has just as much to do with YOUR SUCCESS, as what you choose to do.

Here is what this means exactly.

What you chose to <u>not</u> focus on has just as much to do with your success as what you choose to focus on.

The Main Thing is to keep the Main Thing the Main Thing. Your main focus should be one thing and ONLY one thing – Have I made a sale today?

How is what I am doing, or how is what I am focused on, helping me to achieve one sale today? Not tomorrow, not later, not when I get "better leads". TODAY.

From day one, while making personal sales from this telesales platform, my only focus was to average **no less** than one sale per day. Period.

In the course of making one daily sale, I generated one or more sales daily. Why? Luck? NO WAY!! The secret to my success is that when I am doing telesales, I am focused on one thing – and ONLY ONE THING – selling one policy today.

This is why I sold 9 policies my first full week of dialing, even though I was not expert at it. To be honest, for the first 9 months, as I quickly rose in ranking to become the #1 Top Producer in our company out of a multiple hundreds sales force, **I was ignorant** of certain aspects of this new insurance telesales business.

In the first 9 months, I could not tell you the response rates of ANY of my lead mailers, or the cost of any of my chargebacks, my contract renewal percentages, my cancelled policies, daily business expense, dials per day, presentations per day, or my daily commission statements. These were NOT my focus.

I focused on one thing – becoming very good at making sales and serving the insurances needs of customers <u>every day</u> .

Because this was my daily focus, guess what I became good at – making sales! I am not good at keeping up with mailer response rates, daily business expense, daily commission statements, dials per day, presentations per day, chargebacks, etc. etc. etc. etc. etc. etc. etc. Why? It is not my focus. NONE of this numerical data even matters anyway, if an agent is not making sales. However, ALL of these things WILL work themselves out, if an agent is consistently making sales.

You can become expert in all aspects of a final expense sales platform, except the Main Thing. *Selling policies is king.*

If I make one or more sales **today**, you'll let me slide if I'm not up to speed on my mailer response rates, won't you? However, if I make zero sales today, yet I know the percentage of leads to mailers for the past 3 months, what gives? What good is it to your selling skill to spend time researching statistical data?!

Is what you are focused on helping you to make one sale TODAY?

In golf, a player is taught to "keep your head down" while addressing the ball at the pre-swing, follow through, and then back-swing. Why? Keeping your head down at all points in the golf swing focuses a player's eye onto the golf ball to make solid contact and a straight drive.

In football, a running back is taught to not only cover the ball with both hands, but to also "keep your head down", while breaking through the line of defenders for more yardage. Why? Keeping the running back's head down maintains balance as the running back is being hit and knocked around, while moving the ball forward.

In baseball, a batter is taught to "keep your eye on the ball" when swinging for the fence. Why? If the pitcher throws a curve ball, the batter may follow the path of the curving ball as it glides across home plate and into direct contact of the batter's swing.

In final expense field or phone sales, you are being taught to "keep your head down" How? Maintain your focus on direct selling. Outside distractions will pop up all around you, begging your attention throughout the day. Will you "keep your head down"? Will you "keep your eye on the ball" and remained focused on improving your selling skill today? Focus. FOCUS. **FOCUS.**

Side Jobs

Agents experiencing an upfront learning curve of a final expense sales program sometimes resort to earning "side money", until they become proficient at selling final expense policies over the telephone. Warning: Failure in rearview mirror is closer than it appears.

Although it is commendable for an agent to choose to work 2 jobs, it can be a losing prospect in final expense sales.

The Main Thing is to keep the Main Thing the Main Thing. There is only **one thing** that will consistently grow an agent's bank account – selling policies by serving families. This requires time on the telephone.

Attempting to sell a car, or earn extra cash on EBay, or pursuing a host of other potential revenue streams, only dilutes your *perfect opportunity* to earn great income by the end of this week without needing to do anything extra. More critically, by supplementing your telesales business with unstable, quick-cash schemes, it prolongs the maturity of a successful, profitable insurance business.

If you want customers to focus on your product, then you must put your focus on serving families.

The whole point in selling final expense policies from the comfort of your own business or home office, is so that YOU DO NOT HAVE TO EARN ADDITIONAL INCOME, right?

Your daily, #1, absolute, TOP Priority as a final expense phone sales expert is to become so good at meeting the life insurance needs of your clientele lead base, until you do not have enough time to keep your record book current with so many sales!

This will create the most fluid and generous income stream for any agent who is faithfully working from a good final expense sales platform in the right way.

Customer Conversation Control

Who should ultimately be in control of the conversation, the customer, or the agent? The agent! Sometimes a customer without a specific need, or who may be overly nervous about qualifying for a plan, will ramble. Endless chatter.

If a customer is prone to "run their mouth" about life insurance or something else, an expert agent who wants to get a word in edgewise or take back control of the conversation, must employ skillful conversation techniques to do so respectfully.

An effective technique is the "Invisible Interruption".

An agent must interrupt the rambling customer who cannot stay focused on one subject of conversation. The subtle way to do this is to add to what the customer is talking about. It does not sound like an interruption, even though it is.

Ask the customer questions about the topic **they** are on at the moment. Whoever is asking the questions is IN CONTROL of the conversation. Now, the customer is answering questions, instead of rambling. The customer will then be following the agent's lead in the questioning. The agent soon will employ a question about final expense protection to bring the conversation back around to the business at hand.

Trying to out-talk a customer by abruptly changing the subject may be perceived by the customer as uncaring. So, rather than changing the subject, ask the customer to explain further their current topic of conversation with an "Invisible Interruption".

An example conversation between a customer and an agent using the "invisible interruption":

Agent: *May I verify the card that you mailed back into my department?*
Client: *Sure.*
Agent: *You gave us your name as Mary Smith. Is this correct?*
Client: *That is correct.*

Agent: *You also gave us your address as....and your date of birth as.....Is this correct?*
Client: *Yes.*
Agent: *OK. Great! Looks like I have the right person.*
Client: *Ya' know, my husband and I lived here for 42 years together.*
Agent: *Wow. Is that right?*
Client: *Yes. In fact, my husband practically restructured everything inside this house.*
Agent: *What was your husband's name?*
Client: *Herman.*
Agent: *What to do mean by Herman practically restructured everything inside the house? Tell me more about that.* **(INVISIBLE INTERRUPTION)**
Client: *Well, he fixed a gas leak several years ago when our babies were young. He worked all night to re-plumb the piping system in the basement to fix the leak.*
Agent: *My goodness, Mary. What did Herman do next?*
Client: *Herman was a good handyman. He laid down new carpet in the entire house after our 3 children went to college. He changed out the water heater into a heat pump unit. He built a garage on the side of the house. His most recent project was making a game room out of the basement for the grandchildren.*
Agent: *Good grief! What a great guy. God bless his precious memory. It sounds like he was an example to his family, and he showed his love mostly through his actions. Is that safe to say?*
Client: *Yes, that's a good way to put it.*
Agent: *Too bad your beloved handyman isn't there to fix things for you now. He's probably working on a guardrail around the clouds in Heaven, so no one will fall out. You reckon? I'm only kidding, Mary.*
Client: *Ha, ha. You're probably right.*
Agent: *I hate to think this way, Mary, but God forbid if something should happen like another gas leak, or carbon monoxide poisoning inside the house, who would take care of fixing for you?*
Client: *Probably my children, John, my youngest son in particular.*

Agent: *Is John the one that I would be working with to pay out the cash benefits to within 48 hours, that is, if something should happen to you, if you qualify for one of our state-approved funeral and burial protection plans?*
Client: Yes. John would handle most of it.

This brings the agent back to an "interviewing position" in the conversation. The agent should be the interviewer, or the "questioner". The interviewer is the one in control of the course of conversation.

Low Productivity Goals

A professional final expense agent should set a goal of being able to sell 7-15 policies minimum per week. Here is why.

Discouragement over policy cancellations or policy declines is an agent nightmare if personal production is low. The reason why low producing agents cannot handle this is because, if an agent sells only 2-4 policies per week, and 1 or 2 of them cancel, it blows the agent clean out of the water, financially speaking. However, if an agent sells 7-15 policies per week and 2 cancel (which is uncommon in one week, if an agent follows our system in the right way), it is no big deal.

Avoid getting all hot and "bent outta' shape" if a client cancels, or a policy declines. How? Keep selling and serving customers!

When an agent sells a policy early in the day, it is good "insurance" to continue on to sell another policy in the same day, instead of unwisely taking the rest of the day off. If one policy cancels, always have a backup.

As a self employed insurance professional, I can never get fired. I work my own hours. I have no supervisor "lording" over my shoulder. I have no quotas to reach. I am not pressured by production deadlines. I am my own boss. Yippee !!

Yet, there is a tradeoff. The much neglected tradeoff to being a self employed individual is that you MUST **discipline yourself** to be productive <u>every day</u> !

This is the business reality that Master Salesmen put into practice all the time. Nothing else matters if I am not making a minimum of one sale today.

Being self employed is oftentimes more difficult than working for an employer, because you must be both boss and employee. More hours are required up front to learn a new telesales business, because an agent must be self motivated, self disciplined, and self taught to improve him/herself to experience daily **results** that a supervisor normally demands.

What are your productivity goals? What do you expect to make happen each day? Low goals. Low income.

Just because an agent is self employed should not excuse laxity. In fact, realize that you may have to work **harder** and **longer** for several weeks before you get the hang of wearing different hats as a self employed expert.

Multi-Tasking While Selling

Telesales while preparing dinner does not work. Telesales while emailing does not work. Telesales while selling on EBay does not work. Telesales while eating does not work. Telesales while day trading on the stock market does not work. Telesales while disciplining children does not work. Telesales while surfing the internet does not work. Telesales while scheduling doctor and dentist appointments does not work. Telesales while planning a party does not work. Telesales while writing a book (ha ha) does not work. Telesales while working a side business does not work. Telesales while tracking commissions does not work. Telesales while requesting lead response rates does not work. Telesales while trying to conserve policies that have challenging issues does not work. Telesales while selling homeowners, auto, LTC, Medicare, disability, health, mortgage protection, dental, or other insurances does not work. Telesales while planning financial seminars does not work. Telesales while cleaning does not work. Telesales while planning a vacation definitely

does not work. Telesales while having a 3-way conversation does not work. Telesales while traveling in a car does not work. Telesales while answering your cell phone does not work. Telesales while texting does not work. Telesales while checking the news does not work. Telesales while checking your bank account balance does not work. Telesales while sharpening pencils does not work. Telesales while reading a magazine does not work. Telesales while repairing sunglasses does not work. Telesales while watching TV, or an internet video does not work. Telesales while looking for another job never works. Telesales while shopping online does not work. Telesales while feeding or playing with a pet does not work. Telesales while doing the laundry does not work. Telesales while flying a kite does not work...Telesales plus ANYTHING else does not work.
Do you get the point, or should I keep going?

Straight Talk on Selling Final Expense

To make TELEsales, you must be on the TELEphone.

To coin a fisherman's lyric:

*You won't catch any fish,
if you don't throw a hook in the water.*

This is the catalyst to serving final expense policies over the telephone. How many times does a fisherman cast his hook into the water without results, before he eventually catches a fish? Several!
What if a fisherman wakes up at the crack of dawn, puts together his fishing gear, makes a sack lunch, slides on his fishing vest and his favorite cargo fishing hat, loads his pickup truck with a cooler of drinks, lays his fold-up seat in the floorboard, buys his bait at the convenience store on the way, gets everything set up at the edge of a quiet pond, casts the hook with bait into

the water ten times, catches nothing, then exclaims, *"No fish here. I'm going home!"* How silly would that be? The fisherman at home analyzes, *"Those darn fish. They refused my choice of bait. They nibbled a couple times, but showed no real interest. One fish even spit the bait out at me! Fishing doesn't work."* The fisherman never even considered using **different** bait, a different fishing spot, or a different time of the day to increase his skill as a fisherman.

How silly is that? Yet, we all are aware that a skilled fisherman who lands fish consistently has become proficient through trial and error experience.

It is no different in final expense sales. How bad do you want it? – to make a sale today?! I promise you there is a sale to be made today. I said TODAY!!!

It makes no difference to me how many numbers I dial, how many people I talk to, how many presentations I do, how many times my "bait" is spit back in my direction (rejection), how many hang-ups, how many "no's' I hear, how many times I have to start over with the next customer.

No matter how many times it requires to throwing my hook back into the water, one thing is as sure as the sun rising in the east and setting in the west – There Is A Sale To Be Made Today! I believe it! Why? Because I've thrown a hook into the water enough times to see its purpose fulfilled over and over again.

Suppose a fisherman says, *"I am not casting my hook where fish have already nibbled at someone else's bait."* WHAT?!? This is exactly where a fisherman ought to be casting the hook. Transfer this mentality to "B" leads.

"B" leads have already been nibbled on by potential customers. "B" leads may be older leads. Statistically, it takes roughly 5 contacts with a customer before a sale is made. Yet, agents with the wrong perspective snub "B" leads, because they have already been worked by a previous agent.

However, an agent with a winning perspective realizes that older "B" leads just means that a previous agent may not have employed an effective bait (personality) with that customer, or fishing technique (explanation of benefits), or the customer has not reached a "5$_{th}$" contact yet (a skillful closer).

Your first contact with *any customer* may be their 5th inquiry into final expense insurance.

According to Call Center research, it takes on average around 5 dials on the phone to make 1 contact. It then takes on average 4-5 contacts to make 1 presentation. It takes an average of 1-5 presentations to make 1 sale, depending on an agent's individual skill set.

This is why I always stress to my agents to make a minimum of 5-8 full presentations per day to make a minimum of one or more sales per day. My record is 13 final expense sales in one day.

View Dr. Clark's Sales Records:
www.finalexpensesuccess.com/career-bio

I personally have never delivered more than 8 presentations before making a sale. A "No" (refusal by a customer to take coverage) simply gets me closer to the next sale!

One sale per day is a worthy goal when you consider the average commission to the agent per sale is $250-$500. One sale per day working 5 days is not too shabby of a paycheck by Friday. This equates to a six figure income annually in an agent's first year.

Five full presentations per day should be an agent's minimum goal. If you stop working after a 2nd presentation, it is because a) you want something good without really working for it, or b) it may be that you need a better work schedule, so that outside distractions do not interfere with your selling time.

Do you have tough skin? How many rejections, "no's", "I'm not interested", or wrong numbers, do you experience in between sales presentations? Sometimes you can make a sale in the first contact with a customer. Sometimes a single sale requires more effort and perseverance all day long!

No matter how you look at it, if a hook with fresh bait is thrown into a pond stocked with hungry fish enough times, the inevitable will happen. A final expense lead is a "fish" who is or was hungry for benefit information.

A final expense sales agent's lead pool of customers is stocked with various kinds of buyers. "A" leads are fish that initially bump the bait with curious interest. "B" leads are fish that have nibbled the bait. "C" leads are fish that have seen the bait and have yet to make contact. A skillful telesales agent "fisherman" does not discriminate when the hook is cast into the lead pool.

A Master Final Expense salesperson knows that at first, selling policies is a "numbers game". That is, if you talk to enough people and deliver enough presentations in the right way, the statistical odds of making a sale are in your favor the more you do it.

Howbeit, when an agent becomes more skilled in selling after many trial and error experiences, serving policies becomes more about not wasting any time with an unlikely buyer at the moment.

An expert fisherman (final expense agent) knows which bait (final expense benefits) lands certain types of fish (final expense customers), how to cast the bait in front of the fish, what to do when the fish swallows the bait, and how to reel the fish home. Instead of a trial and error "numbers game", it becomes more about specific technique employed for a specific type of fish.

One thing remains the same. Whether you are a beginner or a seasoned pro,

You won't catch any fish,
if you don't throw a hook in the water.

YOU Are The Product

Watch Dr. Clark's Video, *"YOU Are The Actual Product"*:
www.youtube.com/user/DrTroyClark

In sales, it's not how you sell the product. It's how you sell **YOU**.

Product knowledge is not the main part of the sale, although it is an important one. The main part is You. Why? Clients are people. People relate to people. People buy _you_. The product is simply a benefit of knowing you. The main focus is on people, not the product.

A potential client will not buy anything from the salesperson, if they do not feel comfortable with the salesperson, even if the product is free. To project a genuine, likeable you is key.

In sales, **YOU are the actual product**.

As a nationwide Top 10 Life Insurance expert, time after time again, I have watched clients buy my product over another less expensive product that equaled in value. Why? Because the client liked and felt comfortable with **me**.

I probably sold more insurance plans based on the strength of my personality than by convincing the client that my product was better than everyone else's. I used this rapport-first approach to create interest in my product and produce 669 clients in my first year in insurance sales alone.

Sales people earn income by commissions. That is, a percentage of the profits from each sale goes to the sales agent. Then again, no sales means no commission. Decent sales, decent commission. Many sales, much commission income. Therefore, the income level rises with each sale made.

For the first 6 months my weekly sales were quite average, closing maybe 30-40%. That means I would write 3 or 4 insurance policies out of 10 appointments (per day). However, I began to notice something. While visiting with potential clients in their own home, I could put people at ease and spark instant friendship by sheer personality. An empathetic ear, a comforting smile, a dose of humor, and reassuring words resonated between clients and myself. I could build instant rapport using my personality and timing instinct.

My discernable strengths and talents began to emerge. I crafted this rapport of personality into each stage of completing a sale. I learned how to make it hard for the client to say "no" to my insurance plans, because of how positively the client felt with me. I utilized my one strength of personality and incorporated it into every step of every sell made.

The appointment setting, the greeting at the home, the "warm up", the pitch, the close, were all treated to my one, basic strength of personality. My closing rate doubled up to 60-80%. That is, I was now walking away from 10 appointments with an average of 6-8 insurance policies sold. I only worked 3 days per week, setting my own schedule, while becoming a nationwide Top 10 salesman for America's largest provider of Senior Benefits. Here is what made the difference. This is a golden nugget of truth that applies as well to any person in any station of life.

Every person is made up of 90% strengths and 10% insecurities. The 90% of your strengths is the real you! Obviously. Now, what do you see when you look at yourself? 90% strengths or 10% insecurities? YOU ARE GOOD AT SOMETHING. YES, YOU ARE GOOD AT SOMETHING! Successful sales people use their strength(s) to create interest in their product....They forget that they have insecurities while making a pitch!

Perhaps you have kept your focus in life on the 10% of your insecurities for so long, that they have been magnified out of proportion! If the feeling of failure weighs heavy against personal success in your life, you are probably by habit keeping your focus on your insecurities, faults, past wrongs, weaknesses, shortcomings, losses, etc, etc, etc......STOP. You are **good** at something.

Perhaps you are good with spoken words. Perhaps you are good with listening. Perhaps you are good with making a first impression. Perhaps you are good with humor. Perhaps you are good with matching needs to suppliers. Perhaps you are good at problem solving. Perhaps you are good at detecting quality in something.

Perhaps you are good with personality. Perhaps you are graced with a natural talent. Perhaps you write well, or sing well, or smile well. USE IT. Use that strength to create interest in what you represent, and produce success with it. This is the real you!!!

Utilizing a strength from within yourself will jettison your level of personal success to heights that will amaze even yourself. You are not your insecurities! You are your strengths, because insecurities are only 10% of who you are.

Remember, people who fix failure change their own view of themselves. This is how it is done. Choose to focus on the 90% of you that is your gift, talent, or strong point. Depend on your strengths to carry you through your situation. Become your strengths. Those who stay defeated by any failure are people who are not willing to see themselves differently than who they think they are. Most well-meaning, good-hearted people deserving success are focused on the wrong thing in themselves -- -- the 10% insecurities.

When I personally realized that I tend to focus by habit on the 10% of my insecurities while selling, I realized that there was 90% of my unused potential toward success that was available to me. I tapped into it, and led many of my peers nationwide in sales, even though I worked far less hours than they did.

You can only see others as you see yourself. Through personal success, the world opens up into a new wonderland of accelerated growth and opportunity.

As I learned in sales, when you can sell you in the business world to clients, your product is bought automatically. Everyone wins. Personal success triumphs. Always remember that who you really are is the 90% of your strengths. Focus there.

YOU are the product!

Like vs. Respect

Almost every agent who sells life insurance over the telephone falls into a common thinking trap of making it a goal to get the customer to "like" the agent. After all, can't the customer just simply hang up the phone, if the agent fails to accomplish this?

So, an average agent spends a great deal of energy and effort during a sales presentation to "win over the customer" by becoming too cozy, or friendly to a disingenuous excess, to whatever degree the agent feels is necessary to make the sale.

This reduces the agent to becoming a "sales puppet", being manipulated by the whimsical strings of the customer (conditions the customer sets for the sale).

In other words, to keep the customer from hanging up the phone, an agent (out of the fear of rejection) places more priority on the whims of the customer, rather than on what the agent knows is best for the situation. A "sales puppet" becomes a sales beggar.

Do not misunderstand. I am not saying that an agent should never care about what the customer thinks or wants. I am not saying an agent should not be friendly. The "Warm Up" page and the "Decision Maker" page within our superior Sales Presentation Script are specifically designed to address what the customer wants and needs in this regard. What I am simply saying is this.

A customer is more likely to make a buying decision from someone they **respect**, rather than from a person they merely *like*.

It is OK for an agent to say *"No"* to a customer. If a customer says that they want the benefit information they requested sent to them in the mail, it is OK for the agent to say, *"No ma'am, I prefer to share the benefits with you that you requested over the telephone, as I am able to now in my schedule today."*

If a customer is too pushy or demanding to the agent, it OK for the agent to stand up for himself! I have had to say to more than one customer, *"Listen, I do not appreciate you being pushy at me and showing me disrespect. I am taking time out of my busy schedule today to respond to your request for our benefits here. Do not ask me again to 'hurry up', please. I am a professional and very good at what I do for people. I want to be very accurate when I give to you the free quote on the benefits you are entitled to. I do not want to feel rushed. If you need more time to receive the free quote from me, then we can reschedule for a better time. Can you not tell me to 'hurry up' again, please?"*

Rather than allow a customer to bully me or reduce me to a "sales puppet", I command respect up front from the customer when necessary.

A customer may not like me standing up for myself, but I have learned a customer will buy **sooner** from an agent they respect. It is amazing how many hundreds of policies I have sold based on having to skillfully "straighten up" a customer's attitude in our initial conversation, before I would then be willing to move forward with the customer.

Conversely, an agent becoming too "cozy" or overly friendly with a customer up front to win them over on a newly-formed-friendship level, as opposed to establishing a relationship of respect upfront, will come back later in the close of the sale to bite the agent.

The "cozy" approach may allow an agent to earn instant rapport with a customer at the beginning. However, if your entire sales presentation is based on a temporary, warm and fuzzy "friendship-shmendship", the customer will sooner back out of a buying decision at the close. Why? A perceived "friend" should just "understand", if the customer wants to put this off, until a later time. It is easier to put off a "friend", than it is to put off someone you respect.

It would be much harder for a customer to put off an agent they respect, who prefers to take care of business today.

Do you see the difference?

Although it does matter to me if I am liked by the customer, I would much rather customers respect me from the very beginning of our initial conversation. I am not trying to be the customer's new buddy. I am a professional. My time is valuable. The customer must get this, in order to see the importance of making a decision sooner than later, while we are both on the telephone together.

To become the customer's "buddy" may earn "brownie points" with the customer up front, but at the close, a "buddy" cannot ask for and earn the sale TODAY, as effectively as a respected professional can.

Predicting the Unpredictable

The surest frustration to an agent being able to figure out final expense sales is to try to figure out the *next* final expense sale. Here's what I mean..

Your next sale is totally UNPREDICTABLE.

Yet, agents focusing on all the numerical nuances, i.e.: lead response rates, numbers of dials, sales to presentation ratios, business expense by the hour, etc., etc., etc., are missing the point of effective selling. This is, in my humble and professional opinion, a huge waste of time and making a big deal out of things that are not really a big deal.

This business is not about numbers and dollar signs! It is about helping people.

I **never** knew my mailer response rates the first nine months of "teleselling", while I became the #1 Top Producer across the country within our organization. I never wanted to calculate or ask upper management to give me a number of dials to sales ratio. Why? Sales are not predictable! I know this going in. How is being a numerical genius going to actually help me make a sale?

Many agents ask me, *"How many hours should I spend working per day?"* My answer, *"Until you make a sale."*

The above agent question comes from a conditional mindset that says – "Well, if this system works, I'll stay on the phone and keep working."

WRONG.

YOU stay on the phone, and the system will work! An agent should never base their work ethic on calculating numbers (number of hours, or dials, or presentations). This is backwards thinking to imagine that an agent should make a sale in "x" amount of time, or "x" amount of dials, etc.

STOP TRYING TO FIGURE IT ALL OUT BY THE NUMBERS !!!!!!!!!!!!!!!!!!!!!!!!!!!!!!!!!!

When you are focused on numbers, then you are focused on merely <u>numbers</u>.

The best motivation for being a telesales agent is the positive, lifelong impact that you are having on the lives of families in need. An expert telesales agent is, in effect, serving grieving people the financial assurance and security they need during their worst week of family loss.

Work on your service skills with customers, rather than your calculation skills with numbers.

Only time will tell if an agent is able to connect with a buying customer. Time on the telephone, that is.

Take your final expense sales system off trial. Stop trying to figure it all out. There is one thing alone that will help YOU make sales today – <u>Talk To People</u>. Dive into the lead pool and apply your best skills of serving others in need – all day long.

When should you expect to make a sale? I do not know. Stop trying to predict the unpredictable. Go to work every day like you would a normal job. You mean 8 hours on the telephone? Yes, indeed! - if you want to be highly successful.

The more people you "get in front of" within our endless supply of final expense leads, the more sales you will make. This is putting your focus on what will help you to make immediate sales.

The only way to predict your next sale is to predictably be on the phone.

An Agent's Biggest Threat To Success

Inactivity on the phone is a final expense sales agent's surest avenue to low or no profitable results.

The safeguard to bypass this threat is for an agent to choose to spend time wisely ONLY on endeavors that bring profitable outcomes.

To know whether or not you are spending your time on what is profitable, simply assess every daily activity with a question, *"How does this help me to make a sale* **TODAY?"**

In the beginning stages, or learning curve, of an agent being able to get their brain wrapped around final expense selling skills, there are several aspects of this business to focus on. Only very few aspects are *profitable*.

I am not going to list all of the viable aspects of this business, because they all do not help me make a sale today ! ONLY activity on the telephone is profitable.

Although I was a National Top Producer selling 14 final expense policies per week "in the field", the pivot that I made to selling final expense insurance over the telephone (telesales) was a brand new, unfamiliar dynamic of selling.

Many are amazed to learn that I sold 9 policies in telesales during my first full work week totaling 65 hours. Most agents only hear the 9 policies sold in one week part of this equation. What is ignored is the fact that 9 policies divided into 65 hours equals 1 policy sold **every 7 solid hours on the telephone**.

Imagine that. Activity on the phone for 7 solid hours (30 min. break for lunch, 15 min. breaks mid morning & mid afternoon). This 7 hours per 1 sale ratio does not include any paperwork, answering emails, or typical office work, etc. etc. – ONLY selling for 7 straight hours(stopping only for restroom breaks and to eat), until a sale was made. Imagine doing this 9 times during one work week.

To be honest, I did not initially know what I was doing. My selling skills over the telephone were not expert at the time I began. I was simply reading a 1-2 page, ineffective Sales Script word-for-word, page-by-page to customer after customer after customer, until I found a buyer.

ACTIVITY on the telephone is profitable. Calculating the number of dials, price per lead, contact to presentation ratios, tracking lead response rates, how many times I was hung-up on, etc, ARE NOT PROFITABLE.

The more activity on the telephone, the more my selling skills increased, and the more policies I sold.

Do you notice the high commitment level of Top Producers now? This is precisely what it takes. Do you have it? Can you focus on profitable ACTIVITY above all else?

Nothing is more important than making a sale today. What good is being an expert in all other aspects of final expense telesales, if you do not make sales? Missing this point is not a minor "oopsie-daisie". An agent must be in the right mindset from the beginning to avoid a thousand different ways to fail.

When asked about my profession, my response is something like this: "I sell money at a discount to people who need it in the worst week of their life." I say this, simply because it is what I **do**.

I am a final expense expert, not because of natural ability, not by talent, no thanks to brains, and definitely not by any luck. **Activity** in *specific endeavors* that gain **profit** is what enables my success.

What is your activity? An agent can predict the doom or growth of their insurance business. Compare your daily activity to:

2 Things That Guarantee Failure:

    1. Not doing what does gain profit.
    2. Continuing to do what does not gain profit.

Agent Sales Tune-Up

In an agent's search for reasons why they are not seeing desired results in policies sold, rarely does an agent look into a mirror. A struggling agent typically is focused on trying to blame then suggest fixing the wrong thing *externally* (leads, script, response rates, product), instead of re-assessing then adjusting their own selling technique.

If an agent's selling results are amounting to less than 5 policies sold per week, may I respectfully suggest that you could use a "TeleSales Agent Tune-Up?"

Your selling technique is the **vehicle** to get you where you want to be financially.

A vehicle's engine consists of many different components. So does an agent's selling technique. Any internal component that is not running well can ruin the entire engine resulting in a fatal breakdown! Struggling agents, even Top Producers, may need a "tune-up" on their TeleSales business and technique, to guarantee that your TeleSales business runs smoothly and *profitably* **EVERY DAY** (1 or more policies sold daily).

Does your selling technique work like a well-oiled, well-defined vehicle engine that takes you from Point "A" (0 Sales) to Point "B" (one or more sales) EVERY DAY?

If not, your FREE "Agent Tune-Up" on the following page consists of a **10 Point TeleSales Inspection**.

Seriously review this 10 Point Inspection. Answer each question "Yes" or "No". To give you an idea, Top Producers answer "Yes" to every question. A "No" answer to *any question* is an exact cause for overall failure to your own selling technique and TeleSales insurance business.

The 10 Point Inspection "No" answers will zero-in on what is **holding you back** from experiencing tremendous growth and **RESULTS** in daily sales.

SELF ADJUSTMENT is the #1 Key to being able to earn $1,500-$3,500 income consistently every week as a final expense sales expert.

Will you self-examine your selling technique and TeleSales business through the 10 Point Inspection? Will you self-correct trouble spots ("No" answers). Will YOU put into practice LIFE-CHANGING steps of adjustment that lead to effective selling?

I began ignorant in TeleSales. I have been where you are now. The 10 Point Inspection represents areas that I changed or adjusted in my own selling technique to get the sales RESULTS that I desire. I am not suggesting any agent do anything in this entire book, that I have not put into practice myself.

10 POINT AGENT INSPECTION

1. Are you settled into a minimum of 6-8 hours **Uninterrupted Selling Time** every day for 5 consecutive days each week?
   _____ Yes _____ No
2. To increase your weekly sales, are you noticeably improving your own selling skill, instead of wishing for "better leads"?
   _____ Yes _____ No
3. Are you following Sales Presentation Script MANUAL exactly page-by-page in your Sales Presentation?
   _____ Yes _____ No
   Is the customer in agreement with you, the agent, on *every page* of the Sales Script before you, the agent, proceed to the next page of the Sales Script?
   _____ Yes _____ No
4. Do you operate your business from the same Weekly Schedule consistently every work week?
   _____ Yes _____ No
5. Do you know which customer objection is "nipped in the bud" on each page of the Sales Script?
   _____ Yes _____ No

6. Does your customer lend to you their bank account information and Social Security number to process their application more times than not?
_____ Yes _____ No
7. If you are ever frozen into inactivity on the phone by "Caller Reluctance", do you get yourself out of it on your own to be able to make sales?
_____ Yes _____ No
8. Can you put everything else going on in your life out of your mind, when you are talking to a customer?
_____ Yes _____ No
9. If you lose or miss a sale for ANY reason, do you continue to make a sale(s) in the same day?
_____ Yes _____ No
10. Are you willing to change your work habits or selling technique IN ANY AREA through self adjustment to see the results you desire in making daily sales?
_____ Yes _____ No

Can-Do Spirit and Final Expense

That which we persist in doing becomes easier – not that the nature of the task has changed, but our ability to do has increased.
Emerson [2]
(1803-1882)

I wish that every person were born into a perfect, bulletproof bubble - a perfect life. A life impervious to the intrusion of negative realities would be great.

On our planet Earth, however, not one person is born into a challenge-free, worry-free existence. Rain mixes with sunshine. Happiness is laced with heartache. Both setback and opportunity blaze the same trail into the future.

How an agent combats small, daily setbacks and temporary failure with a "Can-Do Spirit" is MONUMENTAL to achieving sales today.

The eternal optimist, who is looking for reasons to succeed, converts daily negatives into positive results, while others who are locating reasons for failure only fail themselves becoming pessimists.

Misunderstandings abound about people who find great success. To most, "they" never had to deal with any negatives. "They" just "got lucky".

Oh contraire.

Nothing could be further from the truth! Successful people got that way by being an eternal optimist with a 100% raw-bone commitment to work through despair, instead of giving up.

To become an expert final expense salesperson, an agent MUST NOT balk at a learning curve of minor failures to reach a consistent level of success.

In order to succeed, your desire for success should be greater than your fear of failure.

Bill Cosby 3

Thomas Edison, inventor of the electric light bulb, was teased by critics, who mocked his preliminary experiments, saying, *"Ten thousand experiments, and you haven't learned a thing."*

"Wrong", Edison retorted, *"I've learned ten thousand ways not to invent the electric light."*

After achieving success from his invention, Edison wrote these words, *"Many of life's failures are people who did not realize how close they were to success...**and they just gave up**."*

"I CAN" makes a great man!

Take final expense phone sales agent, Melton, for example:

Melton is 23 years old at the writing of this book. Being legally blind from birth, Melton was struck once by a car. He has diabetes. Melton is also a cancer survivor. Yet, Melton is a Top Producer of final expense sales working out of a Call Center environment. He is an inspiration to us all.

Melton can only see 1-6 inches from his face. He wears special, thick eyeglasses that enable him to read a computer screen 1½ inches from his face. Melton lives 25 miles from the Call Center where he works, and has to secure a ride to work every single day.

In sheer determination, Melton passed his Life Insurance license on the first try. To stay competitive thereafter, Melton **MEMORIZED** a 30 page Sales Script that most agents working in the Call Center read to their customers over the telephone.

There are a number of things that a final expense sales agent is doing in the background, while speaking directly to a customer on the phone, i.e.: writing down or typing customer information (contact info., medical history, prescriptions, existing coverage, etc.), putting together a free quote, beneficiary info., etc. etc. etc. An agent is busy doing all of this, while the customer is speaking on the opposite end of the telephone. Melton must accomplish all of this being legally blind.

The first 5 weeks of Melton's employment yielded 0 policies sold. No production. Zippo. The situation looked bleak for Melton. Yet, he kept on trying to improve his selling skill, working from early morning, until management turned out the lights of the Call Center to close up shop around 9pm. Melton would still be on the phone trying to make a sale!! Melton had to be literally "pried from the telephone" and ordered to stop working!

This illustrates a CAN-DO SPIRIT at its best.

Finally, Melton made his first sale in week #5. His first successful full selling week, Melton sold 8 policies. The week following, Melton sold 12 policies. Many of these sales came from converting older "B" leads into policies sold.

Melton says that he keeps his daily focus on the privilege of helping other people, and the opportunity to employ himself in a stalemate economy of lost jobs. The eye of his spirit is focused on opportunity and reasons to succeed. Melton remains focused on what he does have control over today, not on what he has no control over in his circumstances. His optimistic focus allows Melton to maximize opportunity, not his setbacks.

Today, Melton is regarded as a final expense sales professional expert, who is admired tremendously by our entire company.

"I CAN" makes a great man!

Calvin is another fine example.

In one day, Calvin most likely set a record for turning a day full of negatives into profitable results. The following occurred in the course of one, hot, summer business day in Calvin's life.

An air conditioner went "on the blink" at Calvin's unemployed brother's house, who recently welcomed their firstborn child into the world. Calvin immediately attended to the situation, since his unemployed brother could not afford a repairman. Uncle Calvin fixed the A/C for his baby niece during one of the hottest temperature streaks of midsummer.

Calvin was summoned next to his ailing father's house, as he would need to be transferred to the hospital. A few months later Calvin's father passed away.

While settling his ailing father into the hospital, Calvin received a phone call. A few days earlier, one of Calvin's two vehicles blew a motor. Being a former mechanic, Calvin previously put the word out to a network of repair shops that he was in immediate search of a replacement engine. With Calvin and his wife having 3 children ages 5-15, one could imagine the complications of keeping everyone on schedule with only one vehicle.

The phone call Calvin received was to inform him that an engine Calvin was looking for became available at a sale price. Calvin had to act fast to secure payment for the engine and pick it up the same day. Calvin secured the engine, and, to save money, transferred the engine to his own garage, before showering and arriving at his insurance office later in the afternoon.

Calvin sold 2 policies on the same day of all the before-mentioned challenges, not from calling on fresh "A" leads, but from following up on dusty, dry, "B" leads that were available at the time to Calvin.

After relating this story to me, Calvin stated that what kept his spirit from faltering during this trying day was that his focus remained on his family, instead of himself. The opportunity to assist customers with their final expense insurance needs is simply an outgrowth of assisting his family's immediate needs. To Calvin, the setbacks all worked together for a good opportunity to help others.

"I CAN" makes a great man!

Todd is a Top Agent who demonstrated our final expense telesales motto at its very best – *Sell From Anywhere To Anywhere.*

Todd was working with a couple of customers who needed to tie up some financial loose ends before moving forward to purchase final expense coverage at a later time. Conflicting his schedule was Todd's family vacation in Coast Rica the same week his customers would need his assistance to close 2 sales.

Did this stop Todd? No way. While vacationing in Costa Rica (no less), Todd telephoned his customers in the United States using "voice over" Skype internet telephone. Todd also was able to access his leads online for these customers and close 2 sales! Next, Todd initiated a 3-way interview call with both clients and the underwriting department of the insurance carrier to complete the standard 5-10 minute "Voice Application". Done. SOLD!

Todd closed 2 sales earning $700-900 commissions, while vacationing in Costa Rica. One policy was issued immediately at the time of the "Voice Application". The other policy was issued a few days following the "Voice Application". Todd's expenses on the Costa Rica trip became a tax deductible business expense!

Todd did not realize what a shining example this would become later to our entire company of telesales agents. Todd reports he just wanted to "get the job done". This is layman lingo for successfully overcoming life's challenges.

"*I CAN*" *makes a great man!*
Obstacles to selling policies become obstacles to your success. Everyone has challenges. They MUST be overcome to realize success. Challenges come in all forms, shapes, and sizes. Life itself is an unpredictable obstacle course. So is a profitable business.

Running a smooth business is not how it starts out most of the time. Are you focused on solutions, reasons to succeed, and improving what you DO have control over in your unique set of daily challenges or setbacks?

May I share some of my own disappointments that I experienced, in my first year of becoming a National Top Producer in final expense telesales?

1. A major, bone-melting, earth-shattering personal life reversal caused me to temporarily move back into my parent's home, while in my 30's.
2. Almost **HALF** of my insurance commissions went to my business partner/employer the first three months due to a necessary contractual arrangement. I had to take a bold stand to change my contract later, so that I could receive all commissions that I deserved.
3. A fellow employee who shared a business office with me harbored a special hatred for me apparently for no good reason of her own. She would later curse me to my face before moving out permanently.
4. A girlfriend I was dating was diagnosed with cancer and passed away in less than one year at age 31.
5. I have no window in my office. It is dark in the morning when I arrive and dark when I go home.
6. Because of the way my office room is shaped, and my office furniture laid out, I sat with my back to the door of the small office in a "backward" position. I always had to turn

completely around to see anyone in my doorway.
7. The only chair available for me to use at my desk was a rickety, ole, secretarial chair that was ready to fall apart and ergonomically uncomfortable on several different levels. This chair was stable only when I did not lean back or did not use the armrests. Sitting perfectly still to keep the chair from falling apart, I sold HUNDREDS of policies and became the Top Producer of our entire company. This was my "selling seat".
8. For 5 months my internet service suffered a slow death. It would go in-n-out while making phone calls with customers, while working leads online, while completing Voice Applications with the insurance carrier. Maddening! We *finally* figured out after 5 months of unreliable internet torture that it was a bad internet router, which we quickly replaced. We never knew what an internet router was, until then.
9. There is a constant buzz in my 1970's telephone headset (that the callee cannot hear). I tried switching batteries, jiggling wires, etc. etc. I do not use it much now, but I can still hear the buzz, if I wear it. I made thousands of dials my first year on this buzzing headset.
10. My car motor died.
11. A close friend of mine became my 2nd business partner. He turned out to be a colossal disappointment to me in business. I had to severe our business partnership.
12. The number keys on the telephone keypad constantly got stuck on the 1970's phone system that already existed in the business office where my office was located. I made 50-80 dials per day, manually, many times having to start over because of sticking keys.

ALL WHILE GENERATING ONE OR MORE SALES *DAILY*!!!!

"I CAN" makes a great man!

My own personal journey to master final expense sales, and become a National Top Producer from this business platform, was fraught with daunting, insanity-laden challenges that mocked my positive spirit almost daily.

Sound familiar to your life?

Libraries of stories could be written of the inconceivable lengths insurance agents go to just to make one sale. Without the "Can-Do Spirit" a Top Producer would never be a Top Producer.

While selling final expense insurance "in the field" I personally set 8-12 appointments each day for 3 consecutive selling days per week.

After following a customer's direction to their home in the mountains, I parked my car on the bank of a narrow country road beside of a rusted-out, green 1963 truck with weeds growing out of the windows. These were my "directions".

I then walked a dirt trail into the woods, until it opened up into…..a swinging bridge overhanging a river 100 feet across and 30 feet below. No joke.

After crossing the swinging bridge (beautiful, but treacherous) with my briefcase in hand, I hiked up a mountain one-half mile to reach my customer's modest home. A satellite dish was perched on top of the roof.

There was no way I was coming away empty-handed from this appointment. I made 2 sales, while this couple berated the current President of the United States at the time, who I voted for. Since they wanted to talk politics, I bit my tongue and agreed with everything they said to earn the client's business.

I was a tad late for my next appointment.

"I CAN" makes a great man!

Once while making a final expense tele-sale, my wheezing customer had a coughing spell that lasted 5 minutes. For some ominous reason, our phone line was disconnected 8 times in 3 hours.

While completing the Voice Application with the insurance carrier, the underwriter accidentally hung-up on my client and me. Again, the phone line disconnected twice in the middle of the 3-way call between the customer, underwriter, and me. Thankfully, the customer was extremely cordial and understanding.

It took 3½ hours amidst the agonizing coughing spells of the customer, a "demon possessed" phone connection, and being accidentally hung up on by the insurance underwriter twice before completing the Voice Application, to make this sale!

"I CAN" makes a great man!

After "striking out" all morning with zero sales, I figured, *"This is not my day."* Nothing was going right. Several people hung up on me. Others cut me off in the middle of a sales presentation to make a silly excuse for exiting our conversation. Early afternoon was no better.

However, I made 4 sales in this very same day after 4 pm. Two of those 4 sales were a husband and wife whose adult grandson initially hung-up the telephone on me 3 times before I was able to speak to the customer.

"I CAN" makes a great man!

On and on I could go about the distractions, and challenges we all face just to make one sale.

My very **first** telesale took 5 hours on the telephone to complete! Everything was new and challenging then.

It is not talent, not natural ability, not brains, nor luck that personifies a Master Salesperson. It is simply the "I Can" spirit to succeed despite all obstacles. This is the primary quality winners possess.

Many men fail because they quit too soon.
They lose faith when the signs are against them.
They do not have the courage to hold on,
to keep fighting in spite of that
which seems insurmountable.

Dr. C.E. Welch [4]
Welch's Grape Juice, Founder

Did you know that before Dr. Seuss, the famous writer, sold his first children's book, he was rejected by 23 different publishers. The 24th publisher, who published his book, sold 6 million copies in the first year.

What about auto tycoon, Henry Ford? In his first three years in the automobile business, he went bankrupt...twice.

In its first year of business Coca Cola Company sold only 400 Cokes.

This one even I can hardly believe, since I played Division II Men's College Basketball. Michael Jordan, perhaps the greatest basketball player ever...was cut from his high school basketball team as a sophomore. [5]

Obstacles are necessary for success
because in selling, as in all careers of importance,
victory comes only after
many struggles and countless defeats.

Og Mandino[6]

Without a doubt, a resilient spirit has more to do with what makes a customer want to buy from an agent, than does intelligence, talent, or even experience.

Remember, whatever an agent transfers over the telephone "in the moment" is how a customer will likely respond to an agent. If you were the customer, how would you prefer an agent speak to you? With a know-it-all intelligence? With slick-talking conversational talent? With a dry sense of experience. Or, would you prefer a cheerful spirit from the agent?

A customer is a mirror image of you, the agent, much of the time. What YOU transfer to the customer is normally how a customer will treat you.

So, an agent's disposition is supremely important. How you feel inside is very important. How can this be personally upgraded?

If I allow negative information to have access to me first thing in the morning, it can take away my positive outlook, and replace it with frustration, agitation, or, in other words, a less-than-upbeat perspective. Negative news deadens my selling spirit.

My attitude can be adversely affected by internet world news, emails (cancelled policies, client bank draft issues, chargebacks), unsatisfied customer phone messages, and negative mail. Guess who can pick up on the effect this has on my spirit - customers – over the telephone!!

This is why I access none of the potentially negative news outlets mentioned in the previous paragraph before or during selling time. If anyone of these could potentially turn my day sour, does it sound smart to you to allow any of these to have access to my spirit?

I will *eventually* open my mail, check email, listen to phone messages, and catch up on internet news, in due course of my daily schedule, but NOT before I make a minimum of 1-2 sales first TODAY. This is a commitment I make to myself.

When my inner spirit is not the repository of disappointing news, my mind is clear, clean, and more likely to positively focus on the customer. A customer senses this, and sales are made sooner.

Every final expense telesales agent possesses a natural strength (ability) over the telephone.

Here is short list of possible strengths:

- Delightful personality.
- "Radio voice" that appeals to the listener.
- Paint word pictures.
- Explanations that breakdown complicated information into clarity for the customer.
- Command respect.
- Psychological profile to "size up" the type of customer you are speaking to.

Build your selling skill upon ONE strength----that which you do well over the telephone.

Figure out what you do well and **maximize** it in your presentation. Use your strength to *add value* to the customer's day.

For example, an agent on my team, Tommy, was frustrated with customers constantly talking over him, not giving him the chance to speak, and basically controlling the conversation.

Through individual coaching sessions with Tommy, I realized that Tommy was gifted with a tremendous "radio voice", which he held back in faint volume. Tommy's "radio voice" came across in smooth, deep tones, reminiscent of the late soul-singer, Barry White.

As soon as Tommy learned to inflect robustly his "radio voice" from the beginning of a conversation with a customer, the customer became mesmerized by Tommy's voice appeal. The customer became more interested in what Tommy had to say, instead of the other way around.

Today, Tommy closes many sales based upon ONE strength that was maximized.

You also posses at least one strength over the telephone. What is it? The anchor to selling policies over and over and over again, lies in knowing **one thing** that you do well, and incorporating it throughout your entire presentation.

The bottom line of a Can-Do Spirit is to gratefully acknowledge every morning, *"I get to help people today! And I get paid handsomely for doing so!!"*

This is normally the first thing that comes to my mind when I wake up in the morning. No matter what is going on in my life, I can always count on the opportunity to serve other people, who need my product, within a final expense career.

The more needs of others I fill, the more valuable I become to them, and the more business they allow me to serve.

Selling final expense insurance is a profitable way of serving the needs of others.

It is profitable for the customer to make one, small premium payment to have the cost of their entire funeral paid for. It is profitable as well for the agent, who is rewarded for their professional care by commissions earned.

Everybody wins when an agent's Can-Do Spirit is maximized into one, personal strength while serving others in need through final expense life insurance sales. I believe YOU CAN.

When losing/missing a sale means making money

Successful skill level in selling policies daily is a result of learning hundreds of wrong ways how not to sell final expense insurance.

In the principle of trial and error experience, thousands of wrongs does make a right IF YOU DO NOT REPEAT THE SAME MISTAKES. Knowledge is profitable.

While I attended college fulltime and worked part time several years ago, an older friend of mine asked me to help him clean his swimming pool on a Saturday afternoon. I agreed, because I needed the cash.

Would you believe after spending 5-6 hours cleaning the guy's pool - on a Saturday no less - he only offered me a sandwich, chips, and a soda? He never paid me, because my assumption was incorrect that it was a paying job. He knew I was going through college, extremely busy, and usually broke. How dare he presume that our friendship was payment enough!

Despondent, I pouted my frustration to a wise businessman who listened to my story later in the evening. This was his startling reply, *"You made money today." "Eh?",* I mused, *"How did I make any money today without getting paid one cent?"* Replied the businessman, *"You learned a new skill today – cleaning a swimming pool. This skill may come in handy some day for you. You now know how to do something that can potentially earn income for you in the future. Knowledge is profitable. You, in effect, made money today."*

My point is this. In final expense sales, I learned one of the most common objections from customers who listened to my sales presentation, is the 'ole standby, *"I need to talk this over with _____ before I make any decision."*

For months, I nearly pulled the hair on top of my head out hearing this common objection time after time after time at the close of my presentation. A full final expense sales presentation can take 45 minutes to an hour and a half, depending on a customer's need. I was missing sale after sale after sale being overcome by this single objection.

Then it dawned on me.

I asked myself – How can I prevent this (objection) from occurring at the close of my sales presentation the next time I do a presentation?

I know!

I'll address this issue **up front** with the customer within the first 10-15 minutes of my sales presentation, before the customer ever has a chance to raise this objection later.

If a customer wants me to give a free quote on coverage benefits, and expresses a legitimate need for the service I provide, I will ask one question strategically, before I ever share any information:

"Now, Mr./Mrs. Customer, before I go any further into explaining the benefits, Am I Talking To The Correct Person? Are you your own financial decision maker? Or, do we need to have a son, daughter, Power of Attorney, or anyone else on the phone with us for you to make a decision? If you see something that you want today, can you make this decision on your own by yourself?"

99% of the time, pride alone props the customer to respond that they need no help making their own financial decisions. Of course, if the customer expresses the assistance of anyone else to reach a decision in this matter, I immediately stop my presentation and reschedule the appointment when the customer can bring ALL decision makers present at the point of our next interview.

Hence, I hardly ever hear the *"I need to talk this over with _____"* routine objection, at the close of my sales presentation! The customer's own pride in being their own financial decision maker takes care of that for me.

Learning a better, more effective, way of doing things through the advent of previous failure, **is actually making money**, if you learn how to work *smarter*. This sales technique of mine was eventually implemented as its own page within my Final Expense Sales Presentation Script MANUAL at:

www.finalexpensesuccess.com/sales-script-manual

Handling this particular objection early in the sales presentation, before it is ever brought up by the customer, has helped me to close HUNDREDS of personal sales.

My point is this, I learned a more effective and profitable way of selling **by missing several previous sales**. Learn a better way from mistakes. Learning gains knowledge, knowledge gains experience, experience straightens out the path to success.

If your ability to make sales is suffering, pay attention to the customer's objection that has you stumped. Ask yourself, *"How can I prevent this (objection / challenge) next time I do my sales presentation?"*

Losing sales actually equates to making more money in the future, if you learn a new skill from mistakes. Just like cleaning my friend's swimming pool for free taught me a new skill, giving many free telesales presentations without making money prompted new techniques and increased skill in selling.

This is how losing a sale makes you money!!

I am not judged by the number of times I fail,
but by the number of times I succeed:
and the number of times I succeed
is in direct proportion to the number of times
I fail and keep trying.

Tom Hopkins 7

Conclusion
(Your Opportunity)

This morning you woke up to an instant sale/instant commission business opportunity. A lucratively profitable final expense sales opportunity can be as far reaching as an entire life class upgrade.

Because of our agent-centered philosophy, I have been able to legitimately earn hundreds of thousands of commission dollars for myself and my family here. The profit center truly belongs to the individual agent.

I have also been able to expand my business horizon into growing a National Sales Team. My marketing and advertising opportunities rock.

If you are building a sales organization, you may advertise your company logo at FinalExpenseSuucess.com here:
www.finalexpensesuccess.com/advertise-here

It is a tremendous joy and privilege of my business career to mentor thousands of agents and share this same opportunity of creating wealth by helping others with you.

We look forward to more explosive growth within our company, in spite of a stalemate national economy! If you desire to grow with us, jump in! The water is fine.

Final expense sales opportunities are making national ripples. Our national presence is expanding into every nook-n-cranny of the United States of America. Growing by leaps and bounds, We have employed agents in almost all 50 states.

We do not want to hold anyone back from reaching their dreams. It is the tremendous privilege and joy of my career to train and coach agents to become Top Producers, who then move on to an override commission opportunity with a team of agents.

ALL managers should have experience in being Top Producers themselves. We promote from within our own ranks of consistent producers. We do not want anyone within our organization recruiting or training other agents before you know what you are doing.

If you, the agent, desire to earn $1,000-$3,500 instant commissions through personal sales by the end of each week, it requires being an eternal optimist and a 100% raw-bone commitment to convert semi-interested customers into instant sales. "Lay-downs" do not count, unless you want to only make $200-$600 per week.

Why spend an upfront business cost to do final expense sales and only sell 1-3 policies per week? If you want to stay at $200-$600 weekly income, Taco Bell is always hiring. Pardon my bluntness.

Are you afraid to grow?...as a professional sales expert?

As a manager, I enjoy passing on a understanding of successful selling to an agent, but I cannot increase your skill set. There is one – *and only one way* – to grow your skill, your book of business, and your bank account each week by leaps and bounds. **Experience**

Remember an earlier quote from noted writer, Emerson? ---*"That which we persist in doing becomes easier, not that the nature of the task has changed, but our ability to do has increased."*

I worked 8-12 hour (selling) days, 6 days per week, my first three months in final expense telesales as an entry level agent. I realize that not every agent is like me, but this is precisely my point:

I do not want the norm!

I want to _live_ my dreams, not just dream my dreams. Going on my 10th year in the insurance industry, as I write this book, I am doing just that.

What about YOU? What do you want? The more you want, the more EXPERIENCE is required.

At the original writing of this book, on a Tuesday, I made 4 sales, working 6 hours, while making 7 dials, earning $1,000-$2,000 in commissions ALL IN ONE DAY. How? Luck? NO!! --- Experience! Believe this or not, I am no better of a sales person than You. I've just been doing this longer making hundred-thousands of dials and thousands of sales ONE AT A TIME.

My point is not to brag on myself, but rather to implore every agent to **never stop** growing, learning, and talking, and dialing, and presenting, and falling, and getting back up, and becoming stronger, through gaining Experience.

I believe YOUR dreams will be realized SOONER THAN YOU THINK *through experience* making a minimum of one sale daily, or I would not be writing this book.

I believe You Can REACH YOUR DREAMS IN FINAL EXPENSE SALES!

Do you?

A word to aspiring managers or Call Center owners....

You cannot grow successful selling skills in others if you have never become good at telesales yourself. If you cannot discipline yourself in personal sales, how are you going to manage others?

Everything that I have shared in this book is exactly what I have put into practice myself *on my own.* If you remain unable to overcome customer objections on your own, forget about helping your team of agents to do so. If you do not know how to work from a weekly schedule, forget training others to do so. If you do not ethically follow the Sales Script and treat customers with respect, forget being able to lead a team in the right way.

We want to promote managers who are able to transfer successful selling skills onto others in a positive and motivating way.

It is imperative as well to treat your team of agents as a second family. We are more than business partners. We are business family.

I trust that you have enjoyed reading about your opportunity to better the lives of others, as well as your own, through final expense insurance.

Our business is not about numbers of dials or dollars. It is about helping people. Do you desire to assist others in need of your professional care within our endless pool of lead contacts?

There is someone who requires your expertise to protect their family's future TODAY! One or more sales per day not only boost your own bank account by thousands at the end of each week, more importantly, it broadens your influence to make a positive impact in the lives of needy families.

Selling is a form of serving.

The more needs of others you fill, the more valuable you become to them, and the more business they allow you to serve.

Perhaps your focus has become too self-centered, if you are not seeing sales results. Keep your eyes on helping someone else, before you get what you want.

Are you focused on the numbers of dials, dollars, mailer response rates, or on helping people?

If an agent is selling from the heart, you will do **whatever it requires** to become extremely good at your craft. If an agent is selling from the head, you will flop miserably.

To close, I would like to leave you with a thought to examine yourself.

Is there any area of your life that has or is causing hardship in someone else's life? You only reap what you sow. Profitable business adheres to this principle.

There is something real about making sure that you are right with family, friends, God, others, etc., in every aspect of your own life before things go well in your favor. Call it karma. Call it the Will of God. Call it the unspoken law of the universe. Call it life's unfailing boomerang. Call it what you wish. *Good things happen to people whose heart is in the right place.*

Lasting success is bred by people who are at peace with themselves, and the world they live in.

Ultimate prosperity in serving final expense insurance will flourish along with your own growth and maturity as a total person.

A lot of times failure in one area of life is linked to failure in other areas of life. Conversely, success in one area of life (serving final expense policies) is enlarged by successes in other personal areas.

Take a long, honest look at any area of your life that causes you frustration and ask yourself, *"How am I contributing to failure here?"* This may reveal some painful, yet true realities about who you have become as a person, that roadblock the flow of harmony and success in your entire life.

In life, you don't get what you **want**. You get what **you are**. The quality of your life today connects to the person you have become. A better life means only one thing – a better YOU.

Dr Clark's "A Better YOU" Video:
www.youtube.com/user/DrTroyClark

You may need to involve a little "house-cleaning" in your business or personal life to release defeatism that contributes to failure. Admitting personal wrong and apologizing, if need be, for specific things that have caused hardship on others, are rarely linked to business advice. Yet, nothing breeds quicker growth toward overall prosperity like making things right in all areas.

Happiness is not about more money. It is mostly about every area of your life being congruent. That is, both my personal life and my business life fit hand-in-glove together, perpetuating personal fulfillment.

Nobody lives well by accident. Living well means more than making superior income. It begins with being open to your own inabilities in life, as well as your abilities. Build your life, career, and relationships on the abilities you posses now. Yet, that is only one half of success.

Also, seek wisdom to acknowledge and proactively improve areas of inability where you have experienced failure. If some area or situation is not right, this weakens your overall ability to enjoy and excel in other meaningful areas.

    Areas of life to consider:
            Family relationships.
            Church life absence.
            Social life chaos.
            Personal vices / bad habits.
            Poor business practices.

Broken friendships.
Restitution of debts.
Illegal behavior.

Life has a way of pointing out personal weaknesses that prohibit overall personal success. For example, if a sales agent catches several speeding and/or traffic tickets by constantly overrunning the legal speed limit, this person may also be "overrunning" and not listening to customers when delivering a sales presentation.

The speeding tickets are life's way of telling the sales agent to slow down not only while driving an automobile, but to also slow down, listen, and interact more with a customer when delivering a sales presentation. An overzealous driver on the roadway may be treating his customers to the same overbearing haste in serving final expense coverage. This equates to policies unsold, even when the customer is a buyer.

Hopefully, after the 2_{nd} speeding ticket, the agent wisely will reflect, *"Is my driving habits causing hardship on others, or my own ability to succeed in other areas?"*

There is a reason why we rarely ask ourselves this type of question. Most people adhere to "reasonable explanations" for failure that make us look like a hero (I fail in one area, because I succeed in another area). People rarely want to see personal inabilities or failures as their own fault.

Regardless, there is good news, however, for those who want to live better than the mistakes we all make.

Failure need not be final.

Your life is not defined by the blemishes on your record. Your life is defined by how well you improve yourself.

Healthy improvement in one area of life will always improve other areas. Believe me when I say that I have put myself through exploratory surgery, on several different levels, to cut out of my personal habits, lifestyle choices, relationships, as well as general thoughts and behaviors, ANYTHING that negatively impacted others, or that impedes my chance to obtain success (to make one sale today!).

Truly, I can say that there is little if anything in my Weekly Business Schedule, or personal life, that is counterproductive toward making one sale *today* within my final expense selling skill.

TODAY, virtually every area of my life positively contributes to my well being, and the well being of those around me, while getting the job done daily, reaching my goals, and fulfilling my dreams!! Isn't this what we all want?! Why then, do sales go well for me, Troy Clark?

One Reason: I am willing to admit where I err when life points it out – whatever it is. Inabilities/Failures/Weaknesses. Correction follows. My inabilities become abilities. I become a better person, living a more congruent life, as a stronger salesperson. Both my business and personal life contributes positively to each another.

Sales then occur more frequently. The end.

Self-Adjustment is the biggest unspoken secret to become a Master at serving final expense policies each and every day.

Successful selling is not about becoming a Master of making a client buy. It is all about becoming a Master of
YOU.

Is there something in your life that just isn't right? Ask yourself, *"How can I become a better person through this?" "How does this situation help me to improve myself and make one sale today?"*

Employ Yourself.
Apply Yourself.
Improve Yourself.

These are the 3 Steps to reach the summit of opportunity in final expense sales. It pays in more ways than one to serve final expense insurance coverage being your best YOU.

I bespeak the utmost happiness to you in serving final expense insurance in the right way.

Take care!

Troy Clark, Ph.D.

*I have learned that success is to be measured
not so much by the position
one has reached in life
as by the obstacles which he has overcome
while trying to succeed.*

Booker T. Washington [1]
(1836-1915)

30 *Important Decisions Loved Ones Must Make Immediately For Funeral Arrangements.*

1. Contact Doctor / Coroner.
2. Contact Funeral Director.
3. Contact Clergy.
4. Contact Cemetery or Memorial Park.
5. Notify Relatives and Friends.
6. Select Pallbearers.
7. Notify Insurance Agents.
8. Notify Newspaper and Write Obituary.
9. Select organist / Music
10. Select Cemetery Plot.
11. Determine Order of Funeral Service.
12. Pick a Casket.
13. Choose Vault or other Container.
14. Select Clothing.
15. Decide on Flowers.
16. Make Transportation Arrangements.
17. Select Announcements/Thank you Cards.
18. Determine Time and Location of Funeral.
19. Determine Time and Location of Viewing.
20. Provide Vital statistics about the Deceased.
21. Get Death Certificate.

22. Provide Contact Information of all people to be notified.
23. Make Arrangements for out of town Guests.
24. Respond to sympathetic Phone Calls.
25. Answer Cards and Letters.
26. Greet Callers, Friends, and Relatives.
27. Prepare and Sign Necessary Papers.
28. Pay for Funeral Expenses.
29. Provide Food and Meals.
30. Choose Headstone.

BURIAL EXPENSES

Social Security pays a death benefit of $255 and only to the surviving spouse. The Veterans Administration death benefit for a surviving spouse of a veteran, if you qualify, is roughly $450-$800.

Funeral Home Expenses

Service	Cost
Professional Service Charge	$500-1,200
Transfer of the Deceased	$175-300
Casket	$1,900-6,000
Use of Viewing Facility	$350-900
Embalming	$200-700
Cosmetology	$100-300
Service Car/Van/Limo/Hearse	$400-600
Memorial Service/Chapel	$500-700
Flowers	$250-500
Graveside	$400-600
Cemetery Charges	
Plot/Vault	$800-2,000
Headstone and Engraving	.$350-1,000
Opening/Closing of Grave	$350-1,500
Special Ceremonies	$200-500
Total	$1,700-5,000
Grand Total	$6,475-$21,80

Other Expenses Often Forgotten

> Out of town guests: travel, hotel, meals.
> Lawyer's fees.
> Unpaid medical bills: hospital, doctor, nursing care.
> Unpaid debts: loans, credit cards, business accounts.

www.socialsecurity.gov

> Various online sources used to estimate costs.

Prices subject to change and may vary from state to state. *www.funeral-help.com, www.motleyfool.com, www.funeralswithlove.com,* U.S. Senate Committee on Aging 2001.

ENDNOTES

CHAPTER ONE
1. Jay Abraham, www.woopidoo.com/business_quotes, Nov.21,2009.

CHAPTER TWO
1. Tony Robbins, www.quotesdaddy.com/quote/48714/anothny robbins, Nov.21, 2009.

CHAPTER THREE
1. Jack Canfield, www.woopidoo.com/business_quotes, Nov. 21, 2009.

CHAPTER FOUR
1. Jack Canfield, www.woopidoo.com/business_quotes, Nov. 21, 2009.

CHAPTER FIVE
1. Type of Sales Call Reluctance, http://mlmattractionmarketingsuccess.com/212/warning-signs-that-you-have-sales-call-reluctance, Oct.19.2009.

2   Emerson, Mindful Practice, Thought of the Moment.
http://drbenkim.com/thought_of_the_moment?page=1,
Oct.26, 2009.

3   Bill Cosby,
www.quotesdaddy.com/quote/85106/bill-cosby
Nov.21, 2009.

4   Dr. C.E. Welch,
http://www.visionradioproductions.com/node/288, Nov. 21, 2009.

5   What People Say,
http://www.visionradioproductions.com/node/288, Nov. 21, 2009.

6   Og Mandino,
www.woopidoo.com/business_quotes,
Nov.21,2009.

7   Tom Hopkins,
www.thinkexist.com/quotation/151243,
Nov. 28, 2009.

CONCLUSION

1   Booker T. Washington,
www.goodreads.com/author/quotes/84278
Feb. 9, 2010.

BIBLIOGRAPHY

Dr. Ben Kim, *www.drbenkim.com*, Oct. 2009.

Good Reads, *www.goodreads.com*, February 2010.

MLM Attraction Marketing Success, *www.mlmattractionmarketingsuccess.com*, Oct. 2009.

Quotes Daddy, *www.qutoesdaddy.com*, 2009.

Thinkexist.com, *www.thinkexist.com*, 2009.

Vision Productions, *www.visionradioproductions.com*, 2009.

Woopidoo! Quotations, Inspirational Quotes, *www.woopidoo.com*, 2009.

Contact Author

Dr. Troy Clark
P.O. Box 805
Southmont, NC, 27351

Troy@FinalExpenseSuccess.com

INVITE DR. TROY CLARK

to *inspire* your event or organization:

Convention
Corporate Function
Leadership Summit
Sales Training Event
Awards Ceremony / Banquet
College, University Guest Lecturer
Company Retreat / Rally
Seminar, Webinar
Staff Meeting
Bible Study
Cruise

CONTACT SUSAN   800.607.2535

SUSAN@SGSPEAKERS.COM

Video: www.FinalExpenseSuccess.com/troy-speaks

Other Publications By Dr. Troy Clark

The Perfect Bible

Made in the USA
Las Vegas, NV
27 August 2021